SPEAKING ESSENTIALS

Jyoti Malhotra
(B.A Hons. M.A., NET-1, E-Commerce)

Published by:

F-2/16, Ansari road, Daryaganj, New Delhi-110002
☎ 23240026, 23240027 • *Fax:* 011-23240028
✉ info@vspublishers.com • 🌐 www.vspublishers.com

Online Brandstore: amazon.in/vspublishers

Regional Office : Hyderabad
5-1-707/1, Brij Bhawan (Beside Central Bank of India Lane)
Bank Street, Koti, Hyderabad - 500 095
☎ 040-24737290
✉ vspublishershyd@gmail.com

Follow us on:   

BUY OUR BOOKS FROM: AMAZON FLIPKART

ISBN 978-93-505712-9-3

New Edition

DISCLAIMER

While every attempt has been made to provide accurate and timely information in this book, neither the author nor the publisher assumes any responsibility for errors, unintended omissions or commissions detected therein. The author and publisher makes no representation or warranty with respect to the comprehensiveness or completeness of the contents provided.
All matters included have been simplified under professional guidance for general information only, without any warranty for applicability on an individual. Any mention of an organization or a website in the book, by way of citation or as a source of additional information, doesn't imply the endorsement of the content either by the author or the publisher. It is possible that websites cited may have changed or removed between the time of editing and publishing the book.
Results from using the expert opinion in this book will be totally dependent on individual circumstances and factors beyond the control of the author and the publisher.
It makes sense to elicit advice from well informed sources before implementing the ideas given in the book. The reader assumes full responsibility for the consequences arising out from reading this book.
For proper guidance, it is advisable to read the book under the watchful eyes of parents/guardian. The buyer of this book assumes all responsibility for the use of given materials and information.

Printed at : Param Offsetters, Okhla, New Delhi–110020

Dedication

I, with due respect and profound privilege, serene dignity and folded hands dedicate my small piece of research program to my devoted and dedicated parents, Mrs. Kiran Malhotra and Mr. Pradeep Malhotra for their wholesome support and their dignified ambience which they offered me to sail the boat of my life on the path of hardwork and determination. I am really very thankful to both of them for blooming my life with their humble ambience.

Acknowledgement

There is a big vote bank of thanks in my whole projection of this project to my worthy parents, Mrs. & Mr. Deep Birla, My Guide, Mr. Parminder Singh Bhogal, Caring Brothers & Sisters - Mrs. & Mr. Rohit Gandhi, Mrs. & Mr. Aman Malhotra and Mrs. & Mr. Sandeep Malhotra.

My heartiest thanks to my life partner, Mr. Deepak Malhotra (husband) and the little steps of my Angel, Ditya Malhotra (daughter).

I am really grateful to be a part of the V & S Publishers who support my research analysis with their expert team of publishing. I am really very thankful to Mr. Sahil Gupta (Director) and Mr. Binay Srivastava for their wholesome cooperation to convert my research program to a complete masterpiece.

Regards

Jyoti Malhotra

Publisher's Note

V&S Publishers has recently ventured into the field of *Academic Books* with the launch of the *Gen X Series*. 'Gen X' stands for 'Excellence in Generation 'X'. The series comprises books for aspirants of various competitive examinations. Hence, following the success of our previous books in this series, we decided to launch a **series of IELTS or the International English Language Testing System books** under this series. The subject has been divided into five main parts which has been grouped into five books by the author, such as: ***IELTS Tech-Academic Module***, ***IELTS Tech-Writing Essentials***, ***IELTS Tech-Vocal Cosmetics***, ***IELTS Tech- General Module*** and ***IELTS Tech- Speaking Essentials*** for the students, who aspire to study, work or settle abroad.

The books in this exclusive Series are written especially for the Indian students who wish to appear in the IELTS exams. Most of the foreign books available in the market on this subject have been written keeping in view the foreign readers and at times, may appear *Greek* to the students from India, primarily because of issues related to accent, grammatical aspects, spellings, etc. Therefore, the need for these books was felt by V&S Publishers and the author's extensive research on this subject was carefully moulded to present it in the form of five perfect books on IELTS, specifically for Indian students.

Each book contains **Skills, Strategies and Guidelines** written in a simple manner. Unique feature of this book is additional content accompanied with the book, available online on dropbox: https://www.dropbox.com/sh/r66pb0qggd0x6qh/AADJzB9pPnDARC9AY71kmpNMa?dl=0. The content here is interactive and illustrative and presented in a manner that even an average student can grasp the contents and master the language easily and quickly. V&S Publishers hopes that through these books, we can offer the IELTS aspirants – **A Smarter Way to Learn Technical English nationwide.**

Scan Dropbox QR Code : 

Contents

Contents

Preface

The book is specially designed to investigate what skills and strategies are required in writing and speaking modules that distinguish the IELTS proficiency levels. There are a number of factors like Word Stress, Intonation, Rhythm and Cohesive Devices, which is required on behalf of the IELTS candidate in order to determine their assessment over four band scales: Fluency, Grammatical Range and Accuracy, Lexical Resource and Pronunciation. But how to attain all these skills is still a matter of discussion. Without understanding these technical aspects of English language, it is difficult for the IELTS candidate to score better in IELTS Speaking Test as this is the criteria for their oral proficiency. In non-native English country like India and China, no preference is given to learn all these skills. Only few study materials are provided to them to memorise the answers. No preference is to be laid in building of Rhetoric among the candidate. The major objective of the book is:

- ✯ Making the IELTS candidate proficient in speaking test by teaching them all the Rhetorical devices like *Word Stress, Intonation, Rhythm, Cohesive Devices, Fluency, Lexical Resource*, etc.
- ✯ All these techniques should be properly designed and provided to the students in the form of study materials.
- ✯ Sound recorder (self-created by students in mobile phones) software should be used to maintain the Rate of Speech in the IELTS Speaking Task 2
- ✯ Speech therapies should be given to the students to twist their tongues in L2.

In 2001, the IELTS interview format and criteria were revised. A major change was the shift from a single global scale to a set of four analytical scales focussing on different aspects of oral proficiency. This study is concerned with the validity of the analytical rating scales. It aims to verify the descriptors used to define the score points on the scales by providing empirical evidence for the criteria in terms of their overall focus, and their ability to distinguish the levels of performance.

The Speaking Test Band descriptors and the criteria key indicators were analysed in order to identify the relevant analytic categories for each of the four band scales: *fluency, grammatical range* and *accuracy, lexical resource* and *pronunciation*.

Speaking Skills Checklist is as follows:

Production Skills, Pronunciation: Rhythm, Number & Length of Pauses, Stress, Intonation, Contours.

Communication Skills: Fluency, Clarity, Coherence, Confidence, Cultural Appropriateness, etc.

Language Skills: Grammatical Accuracy, Grammatical Range, Vocabulary

But how an IELTS student will build these skills is still the matter of discussion. The IELTS Books/Instructors or even the organization of IELTS are silent in this matter. No doubt, we can get this matter by netsurfing over different websites but what about the authenticity of the study material. The main problem in a non –native English country like India is that how students twist their tongues in L2 (English language) because while learning, they automatically get the influence of L1 (Mother Tongue) because it is their native language, and this is natural, so nobody can avoid it. But learning global (English) language with the help of Vocal Cosmetics/Rhetorical Devices will improve their tongue twisting into L2 (Second Language Acquisition) which automatically improve the proficiency of the candidate in the IELTS Speaking and Writing Test.

Keeping this viewpoint in mind, I have decided to put forth some technical aspects of learning, writing and speaking English through the medium of this book.This will truly help the students to speak good and perfect English.

ABSTRACT

INTERVIEW SESSION

In this part, simple warm up questions based on candidates names, place of residence, leisure, preference, etc. are asked. It consists of 7 to 8 questions. This part covers the most popular 50 Interview Questions which are generally asked by the IELTS instructors. In exam this section is divided into two categories, i.e., phase A & Phase B. Phase A has 4 questions which are related to Hometown, study & work & Phase B has another 4 questions related to Leisure, Hobbies, Food, Friendship, Shopping etc.

Chapter 1 : Interview Session

MOST POPULAR 50 QUESTIONS (INTERVIEW SESSION)

INTERVIEW SESSION

1. **What is your full name ? What should I call you?**

Ans. My name is …… Ankit Bhardwaj. You can simply call me ANKIT.

2. **Can I see your ID?**

Ans. Sure …. Please.

FAMILY

3. **Tell me something about your family?**

Ans. Well….. I belong to a simple, small and nuclear family. I am living with adorable parents and two small sisters. All coordinate with one another and live happily. I must say God has blessed me with "A CLOSE KNIT FAMILY"

4. **What do you like doing most with your family?**

Ans. I like to have long meals, amusement, fun and frolic, would like to tease my sisters, sharing griefs and sorrows with them. These is a common saying – "The family which eats together, lives together and laughs together is truly a close knit family."

5. **Who are close to you in your family?**

Ans. Well… I am very close to my mother, "A true picture of maternity". She cooks what I wish to eat. She loves and teaches me what is good or bad for me. She is really a very virtuous lady with the blend of passionate feelings of a child. I wish to salute this real role model and admire this wonderful creation of God on this planet.

6. **In what way is your family important to you?**

Ans. My family is everything to me. My family members are my best friends and they support me in every real challenge of my life. I know they are always with me, no matter what. They are not only my best friends, but we truly are tied with strong bonds of respect, unity and strength. That's why I used to say my family is my real earned wealth and strength.

WORK

7. Do you work or are you a student?

Ans. I am a very hardworking person. Presently, I am doing both the tasks simultaneously. In the morning hours, I usually go for my orientation classes of language as I am fond of learning linguistics and in the afternoon, I am working as an executive in a reputed company.

8. What are your responsibilities at work ?

Ans. My responsibilities include keeping an eye upon the junior executives for maintaining organisational goals and objectives and so keeping supervision over them, checking their targets as well as maintain coordination and proper communication is my main work. Thorough commitment to work is my first and last responsibility towards work.

STUDY

9. Do you work or are you a student?

Ans. I am a student at the moment. I am studying English Linguistics and literature together and hoping to get more and more excellence in this field.

10. Why do you choose that course or job?

Ans. Honestly speaking, as everyone knows English is a global language. It serves both socially as well as professionally. Because what I believe socially, it is the order of the day and professionally it is 'A Bag of Handsome Perks & Incentives.'

11. What is the most difficult thing about your studies or job?

Ans. The most difficult thing about my studies is its grammatical rules and lexical part. Its really difficult to remember high profile words and proverbs. Moreover, grammatical rules limits my tendency to learn the things.

12. What type of study most of the students prefer these days?

Ans. Very interesting question, see...... The ultimate goal of every education is to earn good, so most of the students these days tend to fall upon more professional studies despite of academic ones. Because these types of vocational studies widen up their empirical outlook and open their arenas for the professional world.

HOBBIES

13. What are your hobbies?

Ans. There is no one thing I'm fanatical about. I have various interests. I am a keen cook and love to make new dishes. I love reading books. I am creative too and love to follow new tracks ever day. Frankly speaking, hobbies add charms to life and pull out the hidden talents and abilities.

14. What do you like about your hobbies?

Ans. Well….the thing that really fascinates me about my hobbies are that it pulls out my hidden talents and abilities. It brings positive changes in my life. It proves to be a creative utilisation of time. It is the best way to refuel your body and mind.

15. What type of hobbies are popular among teenagers in your country?

Ans. Actually, hobbies are personal tastes of every individual. As far as my country's teenage hobbies are concerned, I must say that among boys hobbies like getting involved with online friends, regular visitor of Orkut, Facebook and Twitter, Net surfing, health resorts, gyms and spa, sending SMS, etc. and among Girls are STORIES, Puzzles, Chatting, Tidbits, Creative Arts, etc.

FREE TIME, LEISURE

16. What are the best ways to utilise your free time?

Ans. A 'Hobby a day keeps the doldrums away.' So the best way to utilise your free time is to get completely involved in doing which you like the most. It is really beneficial for everyone to cultivate a suitable hobby to help in the proper channelization of free time.

17. Do people have more free time now than in the past?

Ans. It's really quite ironical to say, as we are living in the gadgetry and luxurious world where labour saving machines, such as washing machines and dishwashers are prevailing yet people are too busy in the rat race of earning and spending money. They don't have time to spend with their relations. But in the past, almost all the work was done manually, still people had time to eat and laugh together.

18. What is the impact of leisure activities on society?

Ans. The impact of leisure activities on the society is spectacular. It becomes a pattern or style of living for the entire society. Everyone follows the same pattern of living and they coordinate their lives accordingly. They can plan their schedules and programmes as per each other's conveniences.

FRIEND, FRIENDSHIP

19. How do you usually contact your friends?

Ans. Well… I usually get very less time to contact my friends, but I always try my every level best to call them or chat with them online.

20. Are friends as important to you as your family?

Ans. Friends and family, both are invaluable and no doubt, both act as a four-leaf clover, hard to find and lucky to have...

21. Do you think friendships change as we get older?

Ans. Very true. Gone are those days when friends used to truly love each other. Nowadays, fake friendships are in the air via various technological advancements like the Facebook or Twitter. Nobody remembers his/her childhood friends.

22. Whom do you call best friend?

Ans. According to my opinion, a Best Friend is much beyond roaming together and sharing good moments. It is about friendship with someone who comes to rescue you from the worst phase of life. Friendship with your best friend is eternal.

HOMETOWN

23. Describe your hometown. (Individual Opinion, because candidates have to answer according to the place where they are residing.)

24. Is your hometown in the grip of problems?

Ans. Undoubtedly, the general problems of my city these days are overpopulated streets, pollution, traffic embezzlements, etc. Some problems shiver down my spine like the evils of female foeticide and hooliganism.

25. What changes would you like to have in your hometown?

Ans. Very interesting question. Well if I am given an opportunity to change my hometown, my first priority will be to provide homes to the slums, then encourage every student of the city to be literate and educated, and last but not least, to bring technical back up for my city.

TRAVEL

26. Do you think it is true that travel broadens the mind?

Ans. I do, yes…it is true. Travel and change of place impart new vigour to the mind.

Travellers never think that they are foreigners. Rather, you see, different ways of living, such as, eating, drinking, interacting with others,etc. allows you to analyse your own culture more objectively.

27. Do young people and older people get benefits from travelling?

Ans. Well ......for youngsters, travelling is an adventurous experience but for older people, it is more of relaxation than enjoyment because while travelling, they get switched off from their regular duties and routine work. Moreover, it is advantageous for both the generation to go for travelling, as it is an eye opener when we observe people of different states or countries and are familiarised with their lifestyles. There's a common saying – 'The World is a book, and those who do not travel, read only a page.'

28. How do you usually travel to work or college?

Ans. Well......The Metro or Bus are the only means of transport in our city from one place to another. Generally, I travel to the place of my work via Metro, as it is the cheapest means of transport as well as it saves time and petrol savvy.

29. Which place do you like to visit the most?

Ans. My country, India is a tourist's paradise. Well...if I get an opportunity, I would like to visit Kashmir, the real paradise on earth. It is a completely blend with natural beauty, ethnic splendour and cultural diversity. It is the 'CROWN HEAD' of India.

ENGLISH LANGUAGE/LANGUAGE LEARNING

30. How do people in your country feel about English being the world language/?

Ans. There is no such feeling in learning the English language. Everyone knows it is a global language, so learning is automatically inevitable and everyone has to embrace this global lingua franca not only for communication, but also for their economic benefits.

31. Do you think the culture of English Speaking Countries as well as the English language dominate the whole world?

Ans. Undoubtedly... I do believe the usage of Internet really allows the scope of English on international grounds. It becomes a trendy language these days. No doubt, these days it becomes the wine upon the lips.

32. When & where you began studying English? Do you face any problem while studying English?

Ans. As you know, I belong to India so English is not my mother tongue... As it my native language.. I began learning this language in my school when I was 5 years old. Learning the English language for the first time can be difficult. However, when done in an exciting and humorous way, learning English vocabulary and grammar are less confusing and more enjoyable.

33. What is the most effective way of learning English ?

Ans. The best way of learning English is to Listen properly. It can be with any source like English Native Speakers, Some English Audio DVD's or CD's, Watching English Movies, etc.

FESTIVAL

34. What is the most important festival of your country?

Ans. AHHHH.... The festival of lights, i.e., Diwali is the most important festival of my country. It comes in the month of October or November. It is related to the Hindu and Sikh history. It brings everyone together under one roof of happiness and prosperity. It provides an opportunity to meet friends and relatives. It strengthens our social bonds. It breaks the monotony of hectic and engrossed life.

35. Can you define festival, how is it celebrated, and why is it celebrated?

Ans. Festivals act like vehicles that carry our culture, religion and history to the new generation. Well, I must say it is an occasion where everyone enjoys fun and fiesta. During festivals, we meet our friends, sit and share with them meals and laugh for long hours. It is celebrated as a symbol of our conventions and customs.

CULTURE

36. Do yòu think the culture of your country influences you?

Ans. Yes..I do... it reflects in your personality the way you eat, the way you dress, the way you adopt different lifestyles, its values & beliefs, etc. It is the widening of minds and spirits. It teaches you how unity can be maintain in the diversities of culture.

37. Which culture is the best, 'Indian' or 'Western'?

Ans. Well... the culture never teaches you anything wrong. It is the thinking capacity of the person that allows you to think this is Indian or Western. The Indian culture is already enriched with values and that's why it is incredible and the Western culture is completely based on Facts of those values, so I think no comparison exists between both of them. Both teaches the real virtues of life.

38. How has your country'culture changed in 50 years time?

Ans. Change is the law of nature, but sometimes, it's frightening to accept the change. Culture does not change because no doubt it is accepted by the society in different ways but its values and norms always remain the same. Earlier, it was limited to customs, but now it is influencing our deportment, etiquettes, mannerisms, food habits, etc. It would not be wrong to say that it is our 'Signature's style' these days.

LIFESTYLE, HEALTH, KEEPING FIT

39. Why do some people think that modern lifestyles are not healthy?

Ans. See, people have a valid reason for thinking so. People today love comfort and luxury, and they want to satisfy their appetites at any cost. Rather than cooking at home, they love to eat out at restaurants and fast food joints. Fast food may be tasty, but contains a lot of fat that is not good for health. Previously, people used to walk or engage in some kind of manual work. That is not the case today. Personal vehicles and modern devices have made their life easy and people have a great aversion towards sweating their bodies. This lifestyle naturally invites diseases.

40. Why do some people choose to lead unhealthy lives?

Ans. The simple answer is laziness. Today many people do not have the discipline to lead a healthy life. They love comfort and convenience in everything that they do. In fact, they don't realise that their comfort and luxury are going to end soon. They need to face the reality sooner or later.

41. Should individuals or governments be responsible for making people's lifestyles healthy?

Ans. It is the individuals themselves who are responsible for making their lifestyles healthy. It is one's personal freedom to lead a healthy lifestyle. The government has nothing to do with it. No government can interfere into such personal affairs. The government can't ask people to eat this or that. The only thing that government can do is to spread awareness about this issue. Nothing more than that.

42. What could be done to encourage people to live in a healthy way?

Ans. The best way to encourage people to live in a healthy way is to spread awareness about the consequences of an unhealthy lifestyle. This can be done through the media like television and newspapers. At an early age, children should be given education about the importance of a healthy lifestyle. It should also be included in the curriculum. Moreover, sports should be made compulsory in schools. Another effective way is to give gym and sports facilities in factories and offices.

MUSIC

43. Which instrument do you like to listen most? (Why?)

Ans. My favourite musical instrument is the flute. (I love listening to the flute, the most). I have always wondered why I like flute. Maybe, it is because of its simplicity or because of its sweet sound. Flute has a very soothing music and it goes directly into your heart. I think it is very easy to learn flute, but I am not sure. Anyway, I like it.

44. Have you ever learnt to play a musical instrument?

Ans. Not really, I don't think I have the talent for it. So I have not seriously tried. When I was small, I just used to play with the harmonium, but actually, I could never play any proper notes. Even now, I love to press the keys of the electric keyboard and I like to hear the sound or the music. But I have never learnt to play any musical instrument.

Children's Games

45. How have games changed from the time when you were a child?

Ans. Games have changed tremendously over the years. When we were children, the standard of the game or the players were not as good as it is today. Moreover, newer rules have been introduced to make it more appealing to the television audiences. I think the speed of the game has considerably increased. There is much more money in sports and games today, so more and more young people are interested in making it a full time career. That was not the case when I was a child.

46. Do you think this has been a positive change? Why?

Ans. Yes, it has definitely been a positive change in all ways. Games have become more popular and players get much better rewards. Televised games have made it possible for people to watch games in the comfort of their homes rather than going to a stadium. Watching games have become a very easy affair. Overall, the standard of the game has improved.

47. Why do you think children like playing games?

Ans. Children are physically very active and you can't keep them idle for a long time. They always like to be with their friends, playing some games. Psychologically, at their age, they can't think of engaging in a serious activity for a long time. Playing games would occupy them in a very effective way; otherwise, they are going to create some mischief at home.

BOOKS

48. What kind of books do you like to read?

Ans. I mostly like to read biographies. I'm not sure why, but it is interesting to read about people's real lives, especially when they have had interesting lives and have had to deal with many problems. I do read fictions as well, but I often find it difficult to get hold of a book that I really like. I also like reading about books dealing with current affairs.

49. Do you read the same kind of books now that you read when you were a child?

Ans. Not really, no. Actually, with I didn't read that much when I was a child, but if, I did it was mainly fiction books, such as fairy tales. Things like The Lion, The Witch and the Wardrobe, and othe such fantasy books.

50. When do you think is the best time to read?

Ans. I think any time is ok, but when I read I like to concentrate, so I can't read for a short time like on a bus ride like some people do. I like to put time aside to enjoy it. So if I have some free time at the weekend, I might read for a few hours. And I nearly always read before I go to bed – this really helps me to sleep.

ABSTRACT

CUE-CARDS

This part covers the most popular Cue-Cards of the IELTS test which commonly appears in the exams and collected from different resources of the IELTs Test with its solutions. Generally in this section, the instructor gives each candidate the Cue-Card with a topic written on it and the student has to prepare notes based on that topic and give a presentation for 2 minutes. So, revise all those Cue-Cards with their Follow-up Queries for Quick Presentation in the IELTS Exam.

MOST POPULAR CUE-CARDS FOR IELTS TEST

Cue-Card-1

Describe your favourite festival

You should say:

– Which festival it is

– Why you like it

– How do you celebrate it

My favourite festival is Deepavali, the festival of lights. The word 'Deepavali'- Deep meaning 'Light' and *Avali* meaning 'row', so its a row of lights. *Lakshmi* (the goddess of wealth and prosperity) *pooja* (worship) is observed in every household and new businesses are commenced, and people exchange sweets among friends and families. They decorate their houses with beautiful, colourful *rangoli* and make awesome floral decorations. On this festival, people wake up early in the morning have oil bath and burst crackers….. This festival is celebrated on a grand scale in almost all the regions of India the other name of this festival is Diwali.

Gurudev Rabindranath Tagore has so aptly put forth the true significance of Diwali in these beautiful lines: "The night is black, kindle the lamp LOVE with thy life and devotion."

Diwali in India is full of fun and frolic and shops are buzzing with people. Almost all the shops are illuminated with colourful light or bulbs, and they offer great Deepavali discounts. So people are very much attracted towards these discounts.

Another Deepavali attraction is the new movie releases and the bursting crackers. In my colony, there is heavy competition for bursting crackers. Usually they get up at 3.30 a.m. and from then onwards the competition among neighbours begins as soon as the day light hits and finally, end after 3 to 4 hours. But to face the reality, today the price of the crackers have rose to such levels people can buy crackers, or afford to spend on crackers. Inspite of all these factors, Diwali is the best of all the festivals.

Follow up Questions

1. **Do you think it is necessary to celebrate festivals?**

Ans. Festivals are the mirror of Indian culture and heritage. Yes, celebrating these festivals are very important so it is essential to celebrate it wholeheartedly, then it brings happiness and prosperity people's lives. These festivals provide more opportunities to meet our relatives and friends to strengthen their social and religious bonds.

2. **How do you celebrate festivals?**

Ans. I celebrate festivals with my parents, siblings and friends relatives. During festivals I keep off from my job and spend the whole day in distributing sweets to my kith and kin.

3. **What is the difference between the way of celebration of the festivals in the past and the present?**

Ans. In the past almost people did not celebrate festivals with pomp and show. Due to conservative and superstitious, outlook they celebrated festivals only at their houses and temples. But nowdays, people become crazy before festivals. They enjoy every festival, whether it belongs to their religion or not. Everybody enjoys it with full fun and frolic. Each new festival comes on the stage of today's world like the Valentine's day, Friendship Day, Father's Day, Mother's day, etc.

4. **Do you think we waste money on the celebration of festivals?**

Ans. Yes, to some extent, it is true, because I do believe that most of the people become extravagant during the festive season. No doubt one should take the necessary things for celebrating festival and performing rituals, but buying unnecessary things during festivals are useless and waste of money.

Cue-Card 2

Describe your favourite movie

You should say:

– Which is the movie

– What is its basic theme.

– How it influences the society

My favourite movie is the winner of the Oscar Award 'Slumdog Millionarire' directed by Danny Boyle. This movie won 8 Oscar awards the related to Sound mixing, Film Editing, Original song and Direction and Motion Picture. Indian music Maestro A R Rahman brought home two awards with his Jai Ho….. composition.

O Saaya is a background theme that helps in speeding up the pace of SlumDog Millionaire with its sheer energy. Heavy on orchestra, *O Saaya* moves at a fast pace and is the kind of song that has to be heard on a high volume to get the right effects. In the film, the main protagonist, a young boy, born and brought up in Mumbai slums without and formal schooling, correctly answers all questions in a popular quiz show and subsequently, is suspected by the quiz master to have won by cheating. Later, in a police lock up and under intense interrogation and torture, he insists "but I knew the answers". The film revolves around the story of how he acquired the 'knowledge'. While the quiz is founded on the expectation of truth through instrumental rationality, Jamal, the contestant uses the strategic rationality effectively. The complete theme of the movie is an implicit critique of the pedagogical model of instrumental knowledge unquestioningly followed in our educational system. This movie is clearly an evident of a journey from 'Rags to Riches'.

Follow up Questions

1. Which type of movies are very popular in your city/country?

Ans. Well… Movies are the remarkable blueprint of every country. In my country, movies are based on social customs and conventions Some movies are dramatic and comical. But nowadays, most of the directions are focussing towards logical, empirical and practical movies which highlight the life of a common man, and is quite popular among people.

2. Do you think movies have any impact on people?

Ans. Yes… up to some extent, I must say movies influence the life of people. It teaches the masses about latest stunts, fashion etc and also makes them aware of the social and economic evils prevailing in the society. But on the other side of the coin, some stunt movies have really put a bad influence on the upon children of almost.

3. What would you like to say about the Multiplex culture in your city?

Ans. The Multiplex culture has really changed the perception of cinema. It really enhances its value by providing more services related to recreation and leisure. These multiplexes are well equipped, air-conditioned and more secure than traditional cinema halls. I really appreciate the new advent of technology in the field of cinema.

4. What do you say about Censorship?

Ans. Censorship defines the boundaries of movies. It has been initiated to maintain the customs, conventions, public secrecy and traditions of the society. It really protects the sentiments of the people living in India who are basically diverse in nature as well as culture.

Cue-Card 3

Describe your favourite bird

You should say:

– Name of the bird

– Its eating habits

Well... Mornings in India are always welcomed with the chirpings of birds. My favourite bird is the Green Parrot. It is different from almost all other birds. Parrots have a strong curved bill, an upright stance, strong legs, and a clawed zygodactyls feet. Most parrots are predominantly green, with other bright colours, and some species are multi-coloured.

The most important components of parrots' diets are seeds, nuts, fruits, buds and other plant material, and a few species also eat insects and small flower animals, and the lories and lorikeets are specialized to feed on nectar from flowers, and soft fruits. Almost all parrots nests are in tree holes (or nestboxes in captivity), where they lay their eggs from which emerge the altricial (helpless) young ones.

Some parrots have the ability to imitate human voice which enhances their popularity as pets. Trapping of wild parrots for the pet trade, as well as other hunting, habitat loss and competition from invasive species, have diminished the wild populations and parrots have been subjected to more exploitation than any other group of birds.

Follow up Questions

1. **How can we protect the birds' life on this earth?**

Ans. We can protect bird's: life by reducing the use of pesticides and providing elements of natural habitat. This, you can create a welcoming place for birds as well as other wildlife.

2. **Are hunting of birds in your country banned?**

Ans. Yes, according to the wildlife Act 1972, Poaching and Hunting of birds in our country are absolutely banned. Any person who is found involving in these types of activities should be immediately penalized or sent behind the bars.

3. **Do you think birds prove helpful for the environment?**

Ans. Yes, Birds are important indicators of environmental health and play a significant role in maintaining the earth's ecological balance. They also propagates plant's life as pollinators. They control insect population. Moreover, in the dispersion of seeds birds play an indispensible role.

Cue-Card 4

Describe your favourite newspaper

You should say:

- What is the name of the newspaper
- What do you like in this newspaper
- How does it become an indispensable thing

A newspaper is a daily, lightweight and largely disposable periodical containing a journal of current news in different versatile topics. These topics include political events, crime, sports, opinion, weather, and many more. Newspapers have also been developed around very narrow topic areas, such as news for merchants in a specific industry, fans of particular sports, fans of the arts, or of specific artists and participants in the same sorts of activities of lifestyles.

My favourite newspaper is "The Tribune". Everyday it enriches me with a volley of vocabulary. The habit of reading English newspapers will help students to improve their language proficiency and grammatical range and accuracy. Many times, certain idioms and phrases are used which make our reading all the more interesting. There is hardly any printer's devil in this newspaper. The most astonishing factor of this paper is that it tries to bring the environment of communal harmony, brotherhood and fraternity. This newspaper never exaggerates things for public. It always works like a true press.

The most important pages of this newspaper are its editorial, science and technology and sports. It also increases our IQ Level. It has separate pages on stock market, satellite channel programs, and movie schedules. Nowdays, this newspaper provide one more supplement related to local news, i.e., belonging to particular regions of the state. This newspaper has really become an indispensable part my life.

Follow up Questions

1. What are the positive points of reading newspapers?

Ans. Reading newspaper daily enhances our knowledge and updates us with national and international news. Moreover, it is cheap, and the best way to enhance knowledge. It is easily available and affordable also.

2. What types of columns are covered by the newspaper?

Ans. Newspapers contain besides news, different kinds of columns such as education, health, science, employment, matrimony, sports, women, children, etc. Usually, I love to reed education and science columns.

3. **Do you think reading newspaper improves your reading skills?**

Ans. Yes, of course, reading newspaper improves my reading skills. Through reading, everyday, I learn a number of new sophisticated words that help me to improve my vocabulary and language skills.

4. **Should a person read it daily?**

Ans. Yes, a person should read a newspaper daily so that he/she might get the daily update of his/her surroundings and the acts which are going around us.

Cue-Card 5

Describe your favourite Animal

– Describe the animal

– Where and when do you see it

– What are its characteristics

I love all animals but my pet dog is my favourite animal. Its tongue is rough and prickly. It has clean glaring eyes and strong sense of smell. The dog is a clever animal and man can train it for all kinds of useful work. It obeys his master or the leader and follows the family rules. The dog around the house will provide protection to tell you when strangers are coming. It helps in hunting and do lots of other work. The dog is a valuable helper to policeman and an efficient assistant to a sportsman. The dog has been called the real friend of man. It is very faithful and affectionate among all other pets. Some people are of the opinion that it is the best companion of man.

Follow up Questions

1. **Why man are cruel towards animals?**

Ans. Many animals are killed for fur, skin, teeth, claws, nails, etc. Some animals are used like guinea pig's fur which is used for scientific experiments. Most of the animals are unhygienic and are not given proper conditions to retain. Due to the cruelties of man towards animals, these species are endangered in the present period of time.

2. Do you think we should love animals?

Ans. Yes, we should love animals because they are the wonderful species made by God. They are very innocent and maintain balance in our ecosystem. Without animals, it is difficult to maintain an ecological balance. Animals cannot speak but it does not mean we should kill them for the fulfilment of our selfishness.

Cue-Card 6

Describe your favourite car

You should say:

– Name of the car

– What you like about that car

– How it is useful for you

Well... Driving is enjoyed by everyone but to drive the vehicle of own taste is different in everybody Nowadays, keeping a car is not considered as luxurious as it was in traditional times. Earlier, it was a status symbol but these days it has become the necessity of life. My favourite car is "Skoda Octavia" The Octavia is well equipped with great technology and unbeatable performance. It is available with various features like a 528-litre double bed boot, anti-lock breaking system (ABS), rear spoiler, alloy wheels, double galvanized body, tilt and rack adjustable steering, and so on. The Skoda Octavia series are offered in petrol and diesel versions with a choice of two transmissions, a 5-speed manual and a 4-speed automatic. The estimated fuel efficiency is 8 km/1 in the city and 12 km/litre on the highway. The starting price of Skoda Octavia is Rs. 11.36 lakh.

Keeping a car serves me many purposes. Firstly, if you have this vehicle, you have also more freedom because you don't depend on public transport and its timetable. Secondly, you can travel and go wherever you want and the cost of this trip will not be so expensive as travelling by plane or any other means of transport. Thirdly, for a family of medium class, the cost of having a car is better than the cost of paying different transports for every trip. Finally, if you have an emergency, you can drive your car to solve your problems.

Follow up Questions

1. How should petrol in the cars be consumed?

Ans. As we all know, the recession period is going on. During this period, it is our moral duty to conserve the important fuels like petrol. We should consume this natural resource by stopping the car near traffic lights and jams. One should clean carburettor frequently and keep in trim order. Moreover, one should move nearly places by walking instead of using cars.

2. What are the basic reasons for traffic jams?

Ans. Traffic jams at one place or the other are often seen. The basic reason for traffic jams are poor traffic sense among the masses, electricity problem because of which traffic lights stop functioning and sometimes, when some political leaders or celebrities visit your city. Most of the areas and market are sealed, due to which the traffic is jammed in the outerskirts of the city.

3. Do you think a license is necessary to drive a car?

Ans. Yes, of course a licence is necessary to drive a car because it gives the authentification of the driver. He/She knows how to drive a car. Otherwise, anybody can drive his/her car in a ruthless manner. Keeping a licence is the basic rule of conduct for driving any vehicle.

4. Is keeping a car a luxury or necessity?

Ans. Traditionally, keeping a car was considered as a luxury item because at that time people were living with very small amounts of money. Moreover, only few could afford it. But in the contemporary times it has become the basic necessity of life. It is indispensable for our houses in the present times. Nowadays, people love to keep branded cars like Octavia, Honda city, Limousine, Mercedes, etc., just to raise their status in the society.

Cue-Card 7

Describe your favourite flower

You should say:

– Name of the flower

– Why do you like it

– How it is useful

Flowers are a proud assertion, or we can say, a ray of beauty which values all the utilities of the world.

Perfumes are the feelings of flowers. Flowers have an expression of countenance as much as men or animals. Some seem to smile, some have a sad expression, some are pensive and diffident, others again are plain, honest and upright, like the broad-faced sunflower and the hollyhock. My favourite flower is lotus. Lotus is the national flower of India. No other plant figures so prominently in Asian religions as the Lotus. Both the Hindus and the Buddhists regard it as a sacred symbol and use it not only in offerings, but also in countless art forms. The lotus is a native to Asia and flourishes in a wide range of climates from India to China. Unlike other members of the water lily family, its large pink or white petalled flowers and leaf stalks rise above the water, sometimes for a considerable distance. As far beauty and in concerned a lotus is one of the millions of flowers. No wonder it is regarded as the emperor of all flowers, a signature of peace and prosperity!

Lotus oil is reckoned as a pretty good healer. Several cosmetic stuffs like deo, perfumes, scents, candles and so on are made up of the lotus extracts. The effects of lotus fragrance can yield you a distinct persona in the crowd. The fragrance and essence of lotus oil are used for the hormonal development of interpersonal relationship between the animals.

Follow up Questions

1. **What does nature convey us through the beauties of flowers?**

Ans. The nature conveys the messages of love, beauty, peace, harmony and endurance through flowers to the whole world.

2. **Why we offer flowers to Gods in the temples?**

Ans. We offer flowers to Gods in temples for respecting and worshipping him. Moreover, it also shows our dedication towards God.

3. **Which flower is the symbol of love?**

Ans. The Rose flower – the king of all flowers is the symbol of love. It is used to express love for each other. The red rose is always in high demand near some special days like the Valentine's Day, Teacher's day or the Mother's Day. The petals of this flower are thrown on brides and bridegroom as at the time of wedding.

4. **Do you think flowers really bring fragrance to one's life?**

Ans. Yes, of course flowers always consist of fragrance or beauty, colour, love and affection in its ambience. It is loved by one and all. One feels so elated and delighted after receiving a bouquet from his/her near and dear ones.

Cue-Card 8

Describe your favourite Reality Show

You should say

– What reality show it is

– When you saw it

– What it was about

– And explain why do you like it

Real television is a win-win situation for everyone, be it contestants, the channels or the viewers. The high TRPs that these shows command explain the advantage they have for television channels. For the viewers, they are refreshing change from the (daily soaps) like Saas-Bahu dramas. The biggest gainers are the contestants who are provided with the right platform to show their talents. There are lots of untapped talents in our country and these shows by extending their reach to the small cities that provide an opportunity to bring out their hidden talent. My favourite reality show is the "Indian Idol Junior" at the Sony channel. Now it is over but I really appreciate 13 rip roaring hilarious kids who entertained audiences as they tried to outsmart each other with their versatile singing, jokes and unique performances acts etc. India's first challenge of wits for kids the 'Indian Idol Junior' judged by the famous musician & Lyrscist vishal & shekhar along with the melodion queen of India Shereya Ghoshal. This show was telecasted on every Saturday-Sunday at 9.00 p.m.

I liked it because it brought the real talent of our country and made the small kids a consistent and improved performer. I pray to God to bless these small gems of our country.

Follow up Questions

1. **What do you say about 'Reality show's on TV?**

Ans. After continuous run of sobbing "Sas-bahu" soap operas, TV reality shows are the new flavour of the season. They are the new spicy flavour which TV industry has given a new lease of life. They have attracted big celebrities towards it as they involves huge amounts of money.

2. **Why most of the Bollywood stars are attracted towards reality shows on TV?**

Ans. The Bollywood stars have turned to reality shows as they give them sense of security, monetary gain and rejuvenation of their sagging stardom. Moreover, they get consistent promotions of thier forthcoming movies.

3. **Do you think reality shows in your country are based on foreign format or concept?**

Ans. Most of the reality shows are highly inspired from the US based reality shows and have earned success in our country, for example, the *Big Boss* is inspired from the Big Brother and *Jhalak Dikhlaja* is inspired from *Dancing with the Stars*. Even the Indian Idol is a *desi* version of the American idol.

Cue-Card 9

Describe your my favourite author

– Name of the author

– His cardinal virtues

– What is his/her writing skills and explain how his/her books influence you

Books are great source of knowledge to man. I am a lover of books. I spend most of my spare time in reading. I like to read novels most of all. It helps me to learn new words and also helps me to gain knowledge regarding the field of literature. Thomas Hardy is the writer whom I like most. My youthful mind has turned again and again to the novels of Hardy. I started liking Thomas Hardy after reading his 'Tears' I was all praise for the beautiful and innocent *Tears,* who went through the difficulties of life in a heroic manner. I read the 'Return of the Nature'. This was followed by 'far from the Madding Crowd'. The *Mayor or Caster Bridge* and the *'Judge the Obscuse'*. Hardy impresses me so much because because he has given me unforgettable characters. I am interested in Hardy because of a man's love for woman and woman's love for man. I also learnt from Hardy's novel that happiness in human life is very rare. I also learnt that man is a tool in the hands of fate. There is some unseen power which is always working to destroy human happiness. Nature also plays very important role in the novels of Hardy. There is no divine spirit in the objects of Nature. His description of Landscapes is a very beautiful. His rustic character provides some fun to the reader. On the whole, Hardy gives the impression of a novelist.

Follow up Questions

1. What are the skills required for becoming a good author

Ans. A good author should be a man/women of positive attitude and aptitude. He/She must be flooded with knowledge and with command over one language and terminology he/she has to use. His/Her ideas should be so set-explained that just in a glance, people would be able to understand what do they want to convey. He/She must be adept in the art of creative writing. With the blending of creativity and skills, he/she can produce a masterpiece for the masses.

2. What are the tools necessary for an author?

Ans. An author needs pen, ideas, paper and knowledge of his subject but with all this, patience and hardwork are required for an author.

3. What type of author usually becomes popular?

Ans. Only Self-made authors would achieve success who write from the core of their hearts.

Cue-Card 10

Describe your Favourite Season

– Name of the season

– When does it comes

– What change it brings in the climate

– Why do you like the season

My favourite season is the spring season. The season of spring is a harbinger of joy. Spring is a beautiful period when the winter sun begins to turn warmer and the days get longer. It is the Queen of all Seasons. The entire ambience blooms in the beauty of this season. The nature around is dazzled with colours and fragrance. Though the spring season stays for a very short span of time, it brings newness to the surroundings. The entire atmosphere becomes bouncy. It brings freshness to life. The weather is neither too hot, nor too cold. Basically, the Nature is at its best during this perod. One can see greenery everywhere as flowers bloom, birds twitter and chirp. People become energetic. There is a good atmosphere and a new life everywhere. During the spring, in Punjab the mustard crops get matured and the mustard fields turn into a yellow carpet of flowers. Kite the flying welcomes this season. In the North, yellow is given prominence. Men and women wear yellow garments to greet the auspicious occasion. Images of God too are decked up in yellow flowers and even the sweet meals offered are prepared with hues of yellow.

Follow the Questions

1. What is the significance of Vasant Panchami?

And. '*Vasant* means the spring season". *Vasant Panchami* is the fifth day of the Magh month which is called the *Magh Sud*. Hindus all over the world celebrate this festival with great enthusiasm. This Panchami is also now named as the Hindu Claendar Saraswati Day.

2. Which colour symbolise the Spring Season?

Ans. Yellow Colour is the symbol of the Spring Season. In this season Sarsaswati is designed in yellow garments and worshipped. Men and women try to wear yellow garments. Sweet meals of yellowish hues are exchanged with relatives and friends.

3. Why does Yellow Colour signify the Spring Season?

Ans. On this day, everyone wears a yellow cloth. It represents the ripening of the spring crops. Even the food is coloured yellow by using saffron. Spiritually, the yellow colour is a sign of proportion and it symbolises joy, intellectual energy and wisdom.

Cue – Card 11

Describe your favourite sportsman

You should say:

- Who he is
- Where he lives
- What his achievements are and explain why do you like him

My favourite sportsman is the famous chess player Vishwanathan Anand, the one and only great sportsman, India has ever produced in the field of chess. Anand was born on 11th December 1969. Vishwanathan, a GM in the Southern Railways and Susheela is chess lover. It was his mother who initiated him to the mysteries of the game and saw his growing interest and skills. It is the dream of every mother that her child should be great one day. Looking at Anand's keen interest in the game, his mother inspired and motivated him which led him to become a *world champion*. Both the mother and son would play chess regularly and 13 years later, in December 2000, this prophecy came true.

Popularly Known as Vishy this tiger from Chennai (Madras) learnt chess from the age of six. His assets, i.e., his lightning speed of play and intuitions saw him through as the *Youngest National Champion* at the age of 16. When he was nine years old, his father was posted to Manila. This was the time he really started improving his skills. There was a television programme called the chess Today in the afternoon, featuring analysis of important games by grandmasters and international master. When he was in school, his mother would make a note of all this and gave it to him. He would also solve all the puzzles that the programme featured and won prizes. In 1983, he won the National Junior Championship. In 1984, he took the first step in the international stage to play the Lloyds Bank Masters. At early age of 17 he would never play for a draw. After becoming a professional, he decided to settle down in Spain, because all major tournaments took place in Europe.

On defeating KASPAROV in 1995 Anand became the world champion. He then participated in two championships FIDE and PCA. Anand is currently rated as No 2 in the world in both the rating lists, FIDE and PCA list. He has been awarded many prestigious titles like Arjuna award, the Padmashri, the first recipient of the Rajiv Gandhi Khel Ratna award, the Soviet land Nehru award, the BPL achiever of the world, Sportsman, "Sports man of the year 1995". Anand holds a degree in commerce and his hobbies are reading, swimming and listening to music. A nice person, untouched by fame that made him great. It must be the gift of genius. He has beaten everyone and won the highest rated tournaments, yet perhaps, we fail to gauge his standing. To conclude he is a man of discipline, self-centered, clear reasoning and immediate insight.

Follow up Questions

1. Which games are popular in your Country?

Ans. Cricket, Hockey, Football, Table Tennis, Billiards, Volleyball and Badminton are the popular games of my country. People are mad for Cricket, T-20 and IPL match. Cricket is not just a game but has become a religion in India.

2. Do international sports events play any role in improving relationships across the countries?

Ans. Yes, of course international sports like, the Commonwealth Games, Olympic Games, the World Cup, Football Soccer, etc., provide ample opportunities to the developing and the developed nations to assure themselves. On international grounds during their interaction, they do not only produce their sporting spirits but also improve their relations over international grounds.

3. What do you think about the future of sports in your country?

Ans. India could never show any excellence in the field of sports in the past. But the T-20 World Cup, medals in the Olympics 2008, World Chess Championships, they provide the ray of hope that the talents of Indian sportsmen are still alive. The need of the hour is just to recognise them and provide them with their true identities.

Cue-Card 12

Describe your favourite shopping mall....

– Which shopping mall it is

– Where it is situated

– What types of items it deals with and explain how it is helpful for people

The tremendous hike in the number of shopping malls in metro cities is the direct result of globalization. In its march towards the 'Global village', the shopping malls are providing with the gusto to move still further. The shopping malls can be said to be as a mushroom growth of international brands in India.

My favourite shopping mall is the 'Big Bazaar' emerged amidst the bustle of the city. It stands at the heart of city, and exhibits a wide range of accessories from clothing to footwear, and crockery to books. This shopping mall contains all and sundry of the household chores. At Big Bazaar, you will definitely get the best products at the best prices – that's what we guarantee. With the ever increasing array of private labels, it has opened the doors to the world of fashion and general merchandise including home furnishings, utensils, crockery cutlery, sports goods and much more at prices that will surprise you. And this is just the beginning. The Big Bazaar plans to add much more to complete your shopping experience.

Children come to the Big Bazaar to enjoy because it keeps the latest versions of video game. Teenagers come here to keep abreast with the prevalent trends; whereas, the adults come here to really shop for their necessities.

Being the major centre of commerce, the Big Bazaar is the best place to study the crowd of a city or a town. Here, we can find people trying different kinds of outfits in front of the mirror, or loitering throughout the mall in search of a favourite commodity. In the shopping malls, we find people from different backgrounds joining in for the same cause, viz. shopping.

Follow up Questions

1. **What do you find different in shopping malls?**

Ans. The most different things in shopping malls is to choose the' best' from the variety of things, and the second is bargaining with the shopkeepers and if they do not accept your bargaining, then you tend to leave those fabulous things in the shop.

2. **Do you think window shopping is a wastage of time?**

Ans. No. I don't think so, because at least one should get the exposure and get an idea about the latest brands, its cost, its quality and its value. So I think window shopping is not a wastage of time, rather it makes you aware about the products available in the market.

3. With whom do you prefer to shop?

Ans. I prefer shopping with my parents, relatives and friends because I think these people have good knowledge and experience of various products and new trends in the market. I have noticed that their suggestions is best for me.

Cue – Card 13

Describe You Favourite Hobby

– What is hobby?

– How does it influences your life?

– Your favourite hobby

Hobbies mean spending our leisure in pleasure. Hobbies show the tastes and personality of a person.

Hobbies are a necessary part of our lives in the modern age. Life becomes dull without a hobby. One needs to change from the dullness of daily life. Hobbies provide this change. Recreation is not the only aim of hobby. Hobbies give us knowledge which we do not get from text books. Hobbies are the various ways of spending one's leisure. It is said that an idle man's brain is a devil's workshop. One should not remain idle. Hobbies should fill up our leisure.

Some hobbies are useful, while other hobbies are harmful. Useful hobbies are gardening, swimming, riding and photography. Some hobbies are very expensive. Only rich people can afford to have such hobbies as photography, boating and riding.

My hobby is surfing on the net. Whenever I like to involve myself in leisure time, I usually go for surfing on internet. Because with 'Net-surfing' I am utilising my leisure time also in enhancing my knowledge. I love to watch or make friends on Facebook. I usually watch my daily horoscope on 'yahoo.com' which really predicts good for my forthcoming future. I am very active and innovative man. I love to create, search a new thing from famous search engine "Google" "Aol" "Yahoo, etc. Not only this, I am a lover of music also, so whenever I am be on net, I usually download some of my favourite and latest songs. I find my hobby very useful and profitable.

Follow up Questions

1. How do the hobbies help us in our lives?

Ans. Hobbies are the best utilisation of leisure time. We recreate and relax ourselves by adopting some fruitful hobbies. The chief purpose of developing a hobbies is to relax one's mind.

2. Do you think that there change in the hobbies of today than those in the past?

Ans. Yes, there are lots of changes. In the past, people had hobbies like gardening, stamp collecting, reading books, keeping pets. But in the age of Wi-Fi, people are fond of hobbies like browsing, surfing and chatting on the internet, computer games, downloading songs, mobile programming, animation, driving for fun and singing songs etc.

3. What types of hobbies will the future generation have?

Ans. As we all are residing in an Hi-Tech age of technologies, so in the coming future, virtual games, travelling in space, making friends online and sharing their lives with them, exploring new things etc. will be common among the youngsters.

Cue-Card 14

Describe your favourite political leader

Name of the Leader

His/her candinal virtues

His/Her achievements and how his/her personality influences you

There is a common saying, "It's beauty that captures your attention; personality which captures your heart."

My favourite charismatic personality which really influences the whole world with his cardinal virtues and with the heart of everybody is American President, "BARACK OBAMA" Barack Obama is an Academician and a US Politican, (the first African American President). He took oath and assumed office as the the first American President January 20, 2009. Obama studied at the Harvard Law College. He also served as the Editor of the Harvard Law Review. Michelle and US President barack Obama are married as a happy couple. An excellent work - life balancer. Obama's sporting interests include the American Football and "soccer" that he played in his early years in Indonesia. He is regarded as a Time Person of the year, 2008. He is basically known for his writings. Obama's first book, *Dreams From My Father* which surely stands as the most innovative, lyrical and candid autobiography written by a future President suggests that throughout his life, he has turned to books as a way of acquiring insights and information from others and as a means of breaking out of the bubble of selfhood and, more recently, the bubble of power and fame. His famous writings, "The Portrait of Black Male" really prove to be an astonishing and amazing the influence on the readers. Much has been made of Obama's eloquence-his ability to use words in his speeches to persuade and uplift as well as inspire millions of Americans.

His personality gives a ray of 'hope' in the minds of people who are prostituted with the title of "Black". His Presidency surely gives freedom to all those, are slaves who within the chains of racial discrimination by the Whites. In other words, I can say his rule really ends the dictatorship of Apartheid in this world.

Follow up Questions

1. What are the qualities that make a good leader?

Ans. A good leader must be a complete package of skills, virtues, sincerity, patriotic and honest towards his nation. He should not forget to fulfill the demands of people who elected him as a leader. He should be a source of influence to all. He must be strict at his work which is related to the social, economic and political development of the nation.

2. Do you think throwing 'Shoe' on leaders in the public is right way to show frustration of a citizen?

Ans. No, it is absolutely the wrong way. To show the frustration towards leaders in such a way will not only disgrace those leaders but disgrace us because we them selves choose them to govern us.

3. What kind of politics is there in your country?

Ans. Party politics is quite prevalent almost, every party tries to mould the voters in their favour. Populist slogans are raised to appease the masses. The party wins with the majority of the number of voters. The leader of the majority party is invited form the government.

CUE – CARDS RELATED TO IMPORTANCE/VALUES/ROLES

Cue-Card 15

Explain the value of books in our daily

– What is its role

– How it is useful

– What are different types of books.

– And how it influences the common man

Books are our most trusted and best friends. When we are deserted by our friends or kith and kin we can have the company of books. The books are our sincere and faithful companions. It widens our outlook and make us more analytical, logical and empirical. Books act as bridge between the past and the present. By reading historical books, one can acquaint themselves with history thoroughly. By reading novels and plays one can cut the boredom of life for a short time. No doubt the pleasure of books can only be enjoyed by a good reader. Not only this, books also stimulate the reading habits of the reader. We can also improve our communication skills by reading good English books. These books not only improve our communication skills, but also enrich us with the latest lexical resource which really helps the common man in day to day life. Books also remove the loneliness of life. When we are reading the adventures of some hero, we get so much lost in the text that we become forgetful of our surroundings. We happen to identify ourselves with the hero. A well read man cannot afford to be shallow, narrow and fanatical in his outlook.

Follow up Questions

1. What are the good qualities of a book?

Ans. Good books are based on virtues. They not only consist of fictitious materials, but also remove all the doubts and negative thoughts from the minds of the readers. Good books are logical, empirical and analytical. It contains every necessary content related to the subject on which it is written.

2. Why should people read books?

Ans. Books enhance our level of knowledge, intelligence and creativity. They provide relaxation. They also enhance our faculty of comprehension.

3. What can be done to motivate people to read more?

Ans. I think the Government can open more public libraries, and can fund some campaigns that inspire people to read more. They should also make some subjects compulsory which require reading outside the syllabus in schools and colleges like EVS (Environmental Science), Physical Education, etc.

Cue-Card 16

Explain the value of travelling

You should say:

– Why travelling is necessary

– What changes it brings in life

– How travelling is necessary for education

Travelling is a very useful part of education. It is a much better teacher than books or even the class teacher. What we see with our eyes leave a deeper impression upon us. History, geography, political science and sociology are best taught through trips and tours. Travelling trains us to the practical side of life. Travelling gives us an opportunity to study the political, social and economic conditions of other countries. Moreover, it widens our outlook. Travelling makes us familiar with customs and conventions of different places.

Some of the prejudices and wrong beliefs about other nations can be removed by travelling. It creates in us the feeling of understanding and sympathy for nation and people have different ways of life.

The importance of travelling as a necessary part of education has been recognised by schools and colleges. That is why educational institution organize educational trips to historical places and also to places of geographical and scientific interest. Travelling enhances the exposure of the individual. Only through travelling, an individual comes to know about the different cultures, eating habits and lives of people. It also increases the IQ level of the individual. The basic cons of travelling is to convert the individual into migratory birds. Once the individual becomes fond of travelling, then he/she would not be able to reside at one place.

Follow up Questions

1. **Do you think that knowledge obtained through travelling is perfect and permanent?**

Ans. It is absolutely right. Travelling gives us the firsthand information about things, places, persons and events. It provides an opportunity for acquiring practical knowledge of men and matters and a person gathers all the courage of life in a more successful way. Travelling is essential for the growth of a healthy mind. It's a common saying, The health of the mind cannot be maintained on the ration of books and in motionless classes within the four walls of a school.' So, I fully agree that knowledge obtained through travelling is perfect and permanent.

2. **What is the difference between travelled and an untravelled man?**

Ans. A widely travelled person comes into contact with numerous persons. He gets a new version of life. His outlook becomes broad and widened. He comes to understand and read the viewpoint of others where as an untravelled man, one who has not travelled is just like a frog in a well. He is self-controlled. He is a prisoner of his set ideas.

3. **Why educational tours are arranged for children?**

Ans. Tours have great educational value. Students can learn much through these tours. They will not have to bother about books, and their knowledge will be more adequate and lasting. Tours play a great role in the general growth of a student's mind and heart. A student who never goes on tour is disassembled in his knowledge about the world. Real wisdom may be attained through educational tours only.

Cue-Card 17

Explain the Values of Games and Sports

You should say:

– What are the different sports and games

– Why games and sports are necessary

– What one can learn from games and sports

– And explain how it makes our lives more exciting and enterprising

Games and sports are necessary to keep us physically fit. Different types of games and sports give exercise to the body and keep it fit. Games and Sports provide a good relief from the mental work. While playing games, we forget the worries of life. Games sharpen us mentally because a certain amount of skill is needed while playing games like Hockey, Cricket and Football. Games help us in becoming useful members of the society. Every game is played according to some rules. Breaking rules means foul play. Every foul step means some kind of penalty. Games develop in the players the habit of fair play. A sportsman loves honesty and justice. A real sportsman plays for the sake of playing. Games teach certain other qualities like team spirit mutal cooperation, etc. Obedience to the captain and coach on the sports field makes a player disciplined in life. There is a common saying "All work, no play make a Jack a dull boy." To keep oneself fresh, one should be in a habit to play games. Games and Sports are indispensable need of today's busy life. As we all know, these days people keep themselves busy in the rat race of earning and spending money. Games and Sports free the busy minds of the people by keeping them fresh and energetic. It makes the person more exciting and enterprising.

Follow up Questions

1. **Is education incomplete without games?**

Ans. Education is incomplete without games as it is necessary for the body to be fit and trim. It provides recreation. As a secret, one feels smart and cheerful throughout the day. It brings the best in a person.

2. **Do you agree with this statement; A sound mind resides in a sound body?**

Ans. Yes, it's very true if a person is physically fit, he is also mentally fit and healthy. A healthy man is always hopeful and cheerful. On the other hand, an unhealthy person leads a painful and miserable life.

3. **What are the effects made by the state to enhance the importance of games and sports?**

Ans. Today, games and sports have assumed a great importance. Sportsmen and players have started choosing sports and games as their cases. It is compulsory subject in schools in most of the states in the country. State governments are given special grants to their best sportsman and players. Newspapers and periodicals carry special section for sports news from all the corners of the world. Matches played at the national and international level are relayed on the radio network.

Cue-Card 18

Explain any source of Media

You should say

– Which media it is

– Why it is Indispensable

– What information it provides

– And how it becomes the voice of the people

Newspapers are the cheapest and the convenient source of Print Media. These days 'Press' become the fourth organ of the government. It is the cheapest means of communication and easy to carry and read anywhere with us. Every educated person likes to begin his day with the daily newspaper. A newspaper is a necessary item like the morning tea. The basic function of a newspaper is *mass communication*. It provides information to the vast majority of people who can access it and use the knowledge for their benefits. A newspaper brings us news, views and comments on all significant events. It educates the public, widens our outlook and enlightens our minds. It plays a very important role in democracy. It shapes the public opinion and reflects the intelligent people's reactions to important national and international problems. A good and useful newspaper is salient pillar of political democracy. It is more active than even a responsible opposition in democracy. It provides political education to people. It is the voice of people. It acts as a bridge between the public and the government. In addition to all these, it also covers all local events in detail to update us about our local region. However, it doesn't provide the real time news like television. Moreover, this medium is for the literate people only. Illiterate and usually blind people cannot access this print media.

Follow up Questions

1. What type of news is provided by the newspaper?

Ans. Newspapers have become a part and parcel of our daily life. Even while sitting at home, one can know what is happening in the world. Newspapers give us a lot of information about religious topics, sports, arts and music and record the pulse beats of the nation. A regular reader of newspaper can acquires a lot of knowledge about public affairs. It moulds and rejects the public opinions.

2. Is press a medium of dialogue between the government and the people?

Ans. Yes, the newspaper is regarded as the fourth organ of the government. It expresses the view of the government on important matters of public. It explains and elucidates the stand of the government on various programmes and policies. It also expresses the reactions of the masses programmes. In this way, It is a very powerful weapon for moulding and directing public opinion.

3. Which newspapers is more popular in your country – English or Vernacular?

Ans. In our country, vernacular newspapers are more popular. For someone reading, English newspaper is beyond the comprehension of older and uneducated people, so they generally follow vernacular newspaper.

Cue-Card 19

Talk about Television, Its uses and Abuses

You should say:

– What do you watch in television

– Why people love to watch television

– How it affects our daily life

Television is one of the most popular sources of entertainment these days. It is better than the radio and transistor. It means looking at things which happen at distant places live. Television teaches and pleases. It has almost all different types of programmes. A television watcher forgets his worries of life. It is quite interesting to see things happening before our eyes. Television watchers feel very happy to see for e.g. a man landing on the moon and the space man talking from the space to people who are sitting on the planet (earth). The programmes for families like sports, news and interviews with film actors are very interesting. We can see big world leaders on the television. It brings films to our houses. Television can be used for propaganda against social evils. Everything which has advantages also has disadvantages. Similarly, there are many disadvantages of television. It can harm children's eyes as they are always busy in watching the various cartoon channels or other entertainment programmes. They don't care for their studies as they take more interest in watching television programmes. Sometimes, they sleep late at night and spoil their health. Sometimes television watchers even don't care for the guests who occasionally visit us when they are watching some programmes. In this way, a sensitive guest is more likely to feel offended. Moreover, most of the television programmes are shown late at night. Children wish to see programmes. They keep awake and thus spoil their health. Students also waste a lot of their time in watching television. No doubt, it is true that people of all ages watch television more often in the past. This is because it is not always possible for elders and housewives to go out to pursue hobbies or other activities. Then the only option left for them is watching television. Moreover, working people are tired when they come back home and they feel watching television as they get some rest. On top of it, television these days shows programs to cater to the needs of all ages and classes of people.

Follow up Questions

1. **What do you think has had the greater impact on the minds of people, cinema or TV?**

Ans. Cinema was the most popular form of entertainment before the miracles of television. With the homecoming of television sets and nowadays, LCDs, and Plasmas, Home theatres etc., have become the part of almost every home. Television has left cinema behind and now with its distinctive coloured features and multiplicity of channels, its impact is getting more and more remarked.

2. **Why is television considered as the basic necessity of life?**

Ans. Television, the modern magic picture box, is one of the chief miracles of science. It delights the viewers. Its programmes include children film shows, feature films, news, speeches, debates, etc. A television viewer sits riveted to his set for hours as the beautiful sequence of entertaining programmes passes before his/her eyes. Today one can tour the whole world and one feels he/she is a part of the entire universe through the television programmes. It broadens a man's outlook and makes him/her an enlightened citizen of the world.

Cue-Card 20

Explain the values of Discipline in Life

You should say:

- What is its Role
- How it is useful
- Why it's declining

I believe that discipline is the most important aspect in one's life. It is the supreme law of nature. All objects of nature, follow certain laws of nature, such as alteration of day and night. Discipline is an indispensable need for a modern student. Without decency and decorum the life of a school going student and college going student is spoiled. We must bear in mind that discipline is unavoidable at all levels – individual, societal or national. An indisciplined nation can make no progress. Even at international level also, nations must observe discipline in their dealings with each other otherwise there will be a total chaos and anarchy in the world.

Discipline enhances the sanctity of one's life. It makes life more reasonable and logical. It also tries to build the character of the individual with the instrument of patience and tolerance. But these days indiscipline is raising their alarm heads. Day by Day discipline is following its declining stage. In schools, students don't concentrate on their academic lessons. In colleges, *ragging* is crossing all the limits of discipline. Not only this even, world is not free from indiscipline due to frequent terrorist rapes, dacoity, etc. In today's world, peace has lost it's gleam.

Follow up Questions

1. What are the different forms of discipline?

Ans. The first form of discipline is self-discipline which should come from within. Through this discipline, we can make our liver brighter *Punctuality* is the second form of discipline which teaches us certain rules and nouns of the society. Good manners and etiquettes are the best forms of discipline. With the three forms of discipline, one can progress in his/her life by leaps and bounds.

2. What do you mean by discipline?

Ans. Discipline means the Timing of the mind and character of a person to observe self-control of habits and obedience to the superiors or an established authority.

3. What kind of indiscipline is increasing among the students these days?

Ans. Nowadays, not a single day passes without the news of a strike in some college, or universities. Indisciplinary behaviour on the part of the student has become a matter of everyday occurrence. On frivolous protests, the students choose to go on rampage. They don't hesitate from burning the national property, insulting and attending their teachers, creating chaos and disorders. Sometimes, it is a question paper, sometimes a question of the cinema ticket, sometimes the issue of fees and fares, or sometimes, ragging. They are never in a mood to take their books seriously and attend the classes in a disciplined manner.

Cue-Card 21

Talk about the 'Internet as Boon or Bane'

You should say:

- Why internet is necessary
- What are its advantages and disadvantages
- How it influences your life and explain how do you prevent your self from its harmful effects

Internet is indispensable for Modern Era. It is one of the most exciting inventions of the modern times. It is a boon for humanity in several ways, particularly, in the matters of business, trade, commerce, stocks, and shares, education, health, personal contract, banking, scientific affairs and overseas information. It has brought about a sort of revolution.

It seems the internet can provide information on almost anything within seconds, using a search engine. One can find information on subjects from Art to Zoology. So much information is available on the internet that one risks getting swamped in a flood of news, opinions and solid data. There is no question, then, that access to so much information can cause many problems, especially for persons to belonging to the adolescen, age. It is blatantly misused by several kinds of vested interests. Sometimes, we hear about people getting duped in money matters. Several blogs are used by terrorists, pornographers and such others. Adolescent minds generally fall a prey to the object of curiosity and impressionism.

People cannot be deprived of the internet because it is an inexhaustible source knowledge for the adults, children, as well as adolescents. Therefore children may be allowed to use the internet under the guidance and supervision of some guardian or father or mother.

Follow up Questions

1. Why surfing on the internet harmful for adolescent?

Ans. The adolescent minds are easily prone to falling a prey to the objects of curiosity and impressionist. They are easily duped by hackers. Moreover in this age, they are physically attracted towards the opposite sex because of which they sometimes or usually watch pornographic sites which bring hormonal changes in their body and mind. Because of these harmful effects, surfing on the internet should be under the strict supervision of parents/teachers.

Cue-Card 22

Talk about 'Smart Skills'

You should say :

- What are smart skills
- Why it is necessary
- How one can enhance their smart skills and explain where you can apply them the smart skills

We all are living in the corporate world and if you want an entrepreneurial success in this world only Smart skills or Soft skills help you to remain in the market. Smart skills or Soft Skills like leadership, decision-making, conflict resolution, negotiation, communication, creativity and presentation skills are essential for entrepreneurial success and for maximizing human capital in any enterprise. When balanced with a good management team and an effective human resource management system, soft skills provide a way to get the highest return on the investment in terms of human capital. While professional skills may open the door of opportunity, soft skills keep you in the driver's seat.

According to my opinion the six steps of soft skills are No. 1 Be clear and confident about what you want, No. 2. Be aware of what is going on around you and inside you, No. 3. Have empathy for one another No. 4. Appreciate what you have and what others bring No. 5. Know your limits and stretch beyond them No. 6. Let go off what does not work. Apart from this, an entrepreneur should also focus on Appreciation for others roles, Teamwork as a key to success, Focus on Outcomes and Process, Continuous Learning, etc. These skills really make you a good earner.

Follow up Questions

1. **What type of presentation skills is required in the corporate world?**

Ans. An entrepreneur doesn't know how to present himself/herself in the corporate world is not eligible to survive in the corporate world. There are --- presentation skills like good voice articulation, etiquette and manners to presentation act of public speaking and conversational skills, logical and artificial skills on the behalf of entrepreneur, update knowledge about the business world etc.

2. **Do you think English Language is the basic requirement for learning any soft and smart skills?**

Ans. Yes of course, day by day the English language is expanding its horizons in our daily life. More and more people in different countries are understanding its importance and utility. Moreover, if you know this language, you can go to the major countries of the world and communicate with people there for the purpose of study, business, sightseeing, job seeking, etc.

Cue-Card 23

Talk about the role of Technology in our daily life

You should say:

– What is technology

– How it is useful for man

– How it affects the society and also, explain its achievements

Technology is a term with origins in the Greek "techno" and "logia". However, a strict definition is elusive; "technology" can refer to material objects of use to humanity, such as machines, hardware or utensils.

The human race use of technology began with the conversion of *natural resources* into *simple tools*. The prehistorical discovery of the ability to control fire increased the available sources of food and the invention of the wheel helped humans in travelling in and controlling their environment. Recent technological developments, including the printing press, the telephone and the Internet have lessened the physical barriers of communication and allowed humans to interact on a global scale. However, not all technologies have been used for peaceful purposes; the development of weapons of ever-increasing destructive power has progressed throughout history, from clubs to nuclear weapons.

Technology has affected the society and its surroundings in a number of ways. In many societies, technology has helped develop more advanced economies (including today's global economy) and has allowed the rise of a leisure class. Many technological processes produce unwanted by-products, known as *pollution*, and *depletion of natural resources*, which are detrimental to the earth and its environment. Various implementation of technology influence the values of a society and new technology often raises new ethical questions. Examples include the rise of the notion of efficiency in terms of human productivity, a term originally applied only to machines, and the challenge of traditional norms.

Follow up Questions

1. **How does technology influence the field of health?**

Ans. Technology is a boon for our life. In health, technology helps in both diagnosis and treatment of various diseases. These days MRI, Lasers, X-ray, Ultra scanning, devices are used for detecting the diseases, etc., at early stages. These days the trend of 'Cyber Chondria is gaining its ground where online health conscious tips are provided to people to maintain their health.

2. **How does technology influence the field of communication?**

Ans. In the field of communication 'technology' is progressing by leaps and bounds. Gone are the days when people used to communicate only through telephone. These days mobile phones and iphones cross all the boundaries of the communication world. It has has typically converted the whole world into a global village. Technology really proves as a heart of communication.

3. **What are the destructive uses of technology?**

Ans. Technology has its pros and cons. If it performs miracles with its IT industry, simultaneously it is also spreading viruses like black worm, Y2K bug, which can really crack the economy of any country. Nuclear, laser and other destructive arms and communication are also raising their huge heads which prove to be very fatal for the humanity.

4. **According to you, what is the future of technology?**

Ans. The future of technology is quite bright in every aspects of the society. The potential and super power extent of any country wholly depend upon technology, it uses. The technology will act as a growth engine of every economy in import-export business, in the Gross Domestic Product, or in the form of foreign investment.

CUE-CARDS ON SIBLINGS /RELATIONSHIPS /IDEALS

Cue-Card 24

Describe your Mother

You should say:

– Her character

– Her qualities

– How she influenies you and explain her as the most wonderful person of the planet.

Mothers are the most wonderful creations of God on this earth. A mother's love is the fuel that enables a normal human being to do the impossible. My mom is a neverending song in my heart of comfort, happiness and well-being. I may sometimes forget the words, but always remember its tune. I believe that a good mother is worth than hundred schoolmasters. Really my mom is a true picture of maternity. She plays an indispensable role in my life.

She possesses the qualities of a malleable metal, wherein she moulds herself to the needs and wants of her kids, but at the same time stays strict and strong (as a metal) to guide her kids as to what is good for them and their future. Her love and care, the ability to work for long hours at thankless tasks without complaining are some of her many qualifies. These days the ability to go out and earn a living for her children has made a mother more fabulous and charismatic! Not only this she is also virtuous lady with a blend of patience, compassionate feelings, the wisdom to listen even though you want to screen a loving touch, a gentle smile, super high energy levels and the ability to dish out the punishments if ever necessary. A good communicator also possesses that intuition that we all hear so often. I salute and admire this wonderful masterpiece of the planet.

Follow up Questions

1. Why do children share their secrets with mother mostly?

Ans. The attachment between a mother and her children is the dearest, deepest and charming in the world. Mother is the only human being on the earth. Her children have most intimate relation. The irresistible love and affection of a mother gives her children confidence to share their secrets mostly with her.

2. **Who is the more important for a man? Mother or Wife.**

Ans. Conjugal life apart, a mother is the most important person far as man, So for love, affection and care for her children are concerned, a mother is always on top. A mother cannot be compared with anybody even with the father.

3. **What is the importance of mother in the world?**

Ans. A mother in broader sense means a *female parent*. A mother is source from whom we all are born on this earth. The significance of a mother is beyond measure. There is no limit to the care and affection of a mother towards her children. A mother is the first nurse to her child. A mother is the first teacher in the life of a child.

4. **What should be the first gift for the Mother's Day occasion?**

Ans. One send his/her best wishes to his/her mother on the Mother's Day. Also, one should discuss with her, fulfill all her wishes as much as possible because every mother needs the love and affection of his/her for this occasion.

5. **Between mother or father, why is always a mother the best?**

Ans. Father sees the things through mind, and mother sees through heart which always gives a good result. A mother can bear immense hardship for children without expecting any return from her children.

Cue-Card 25

Describe your Father

You should say about:

– His childhood days
– His qualities
– His experience

"A father is a fellow who has replaced the currency in his wallet with the snapshots of his kids." Only good fathers make good sons. I really love my father very much. He makes our life heaven by ruining himself in the hell. During his own childhood, he faced so many hardships because of which he has become so experienced in tackling my problems. He has a ready answer of my every hardship. He is very hardworking and efficient person. His charisma and virtuousness influences me and encourages me to do something innovative and creative. Not only this, he is also willing to help my mom in the kitchen and household activities. Sometimes he scolds me for my wrong deeds.

He orients my path towards my goals and targets. He is very kind, gentle and patient man. He is a man of letters with many talented features. He always observes me and give proper attention even if he is so tired. I really enjoy the company of my father.

Follow up Questions

1. **What are the qualities of a good father?**

Ans. A good father is one who takes proper care of his children, gives them proper education and guidance to become a successful person in the future. Apart from taking care of his children, a father is a preacher and teacher. He is a good listener and honours his children's feelings. Children see the world through their father's eyes. He is the role model for them.

2. **Why does a father not cherish fatherhood, as much as a mother cherishes motherhood?**

Ans. It is wrong to say that a father doesn't cherish fatherhood. A father knows his responsibilities towards his children. He loves them and fulfills all their requirements of life. He is more accurate in external work and not seem much in the house. He doesn't show so much love as shown by the mother looking after her children the whole day. That doesn't mean that the father doesn't care or love his children. The father works day and night to fulfill all the needs of children, such as education household items and other economic and family needs and problems. He loves in a unique way.

3. **Is it necessary to have a 'god father' to reach at the heights of your glory?**

Ans. Yes, to reach the heights of glory and success, It is necessary to have a God Father. He makes the grooming forces more simple and meticulous. God father is just like a *torchbearer,* who helps us in garnering, spotting and providing opportunities in life as it will curtail our precious years of struggling and steering for gods.

Cue-Card 26

Describe your Brother

You should say about:

– His character

– His qualities

– How he helps you and influences you

It takes two men to make one brother. There is a common saying 'There's no other love like the love from a brother'. My brother is a friend given by nature whom I love dearly from the core of my heart. He always stands by me in my thick and thin. I always share my problems with him. He advises me in my daily life.

He enlightens and guides me spiritually and morally. He always thinks, "we" and no to "I". He is able to listen as well as talk to anyone in the fraternity. He is able to give of himself without expecting something in return.

The thing which I really admire about him is he always treats me like a baby and decides with whom I can go out with he scares away all the "hot guys," he actually stops talking to his friends to talk to me, he tells my mom when I do something wrong, he actually makes me laugh and takes time to annoy me but when he is not there anymore… I'll beg for him to take care of me and annoy me again. These are some of the things of my brother that makes him as my true possession and boon gifted by God.

Cue-Card 27

Describe your Sister

You should say about:

- Her noble qualities
- Her uniqueness
- How she influences your life

Sisters are like different flowers from the garden. There can be no situation in life which the conversation of my dear sister will not administer some comfort to me. My sister is a forever friend to me. I usually feel sweet is the voice of a sister in the season of sorrow. When mom and dad don't understand, a sister always does. My sister is a gift to the heart, a friend to the spirit, and is a golden thread to the scent and smell.

My sister has all the qualities for a contemporary lifestyle with a broad-minded outlook. She is sincere and career-oriented girl, who wants to achieve certain professional success. She has firm Indian, traditional beliefs and understands the importance of a well-balanced lifestyle. She completed her MBA from Australia and is working in the Banking Insurance industry currently. She is sensitive to other's feelings and tries to make sure that people around her are blessed with her presence. She is not materialistic. She is God fearing by nature. Really, she acts as a blossom in the garden of our lives.

Follow up Questions

1. What is sibling rivalry?

Ans. Sibling rivalry is small trifles between brother/sister that results in physical fighting, verbal hostility, teasing or bullying.

2. What causes sibling rivalry?

Ans. The sibling rivalry comes from competition for parental attention, love and approval.

Sibling rivalry is also affected by the pressure in the family of a special needs child, divorce or other family trauma and ethnic and cultural attitudes towards family relationships.

3. Is there any special occasion in your country to mark the relationship between the siblings?

Ans. *Raksha Bandhan,* the bond of protection in Hindi is a Hindu festival, which celebrates the relationship between brothers and sisters. It's celebrated on the full moon of the month of *Shravana.* The festival is marked by the tying of *Rakhi* or holy thread by the sister on the wrist of her brother. The elder brother in return offers a gift to his sister and vows to look after her as a elder sister.

4. What are your responsibilities towards your brother and sisters?

Ans. My responsibility towards my brothers/sisters are that I will always stop them going on the wrong path and advise them what is right or wrong. I will always be in their house of need. I should be their role models, set an example of manners and etiquettes, behaviour. I must always assist them at the time of need I will be a morale booster and a friend, guide and philosopher for my brother and sisters.

Cue-Card 28

Describe your Wife

You should say about:

- Why wife is important in one's life
- Her qualities
- Her indispensable role in a husband's life

Behind every successful man is a woman. 'A good wife makes a good husband'.

Of all the home remedies, 'a good wife is the best'. No man succeeds without a good woman behind him. Wife or mother, if it is both, he is twice blessed indeed." One of my wife's good quality (I should say is her contributions to our family) is her role in managing my house and raising our children. During the formative period of our children, I had to undergo a number of transfers with the change of Head Quarters in my service. That was a period when I underwent transfer every year. I used to take my family along with me each time.

As a result, our children had to change their schools every year. For example, my elder son had to attend 14 schools during his study from class IV to class X. Likewise, my other children (we have 3 children) too, the same fate with them. It looks like impossible, but true. My wife took all pains to keep peace and harmony in the family all the time. However, by the grace of God, my wife's care and efforts all our children are now well-placed. My elder son and the daughter are doctors and the younger son is a computer engineer. This is because of the hard work, love and care (contribution) of my wife. I is the reason, we are still united. I have realised it quite often that without her in my life, would be meaningless and this particular feeling has made me feel that this lady is truly indispensable in my life.

Follow up Questions

1. What things should a husband do to keep his wife happy?

Ans. A husband should take care of his wife like he should speak with her with good manners, take care of her health and if she is not feeling well, he should help her to handle the work. Respect her parents, give her respect, encourage and support for her, etc.

2. Can you define a good wife?

Ans. A good wife always understands her husband, cares him his health, his food and his happiness. Mostly dwelling on his physical comforts is pleasurable to her too, but she should not forget to be with him to support him when the entire world fails him. At that time, her paramount duty is to walk with him as a friend and companion without nagging him.

Cue-Card 29

Describe your Grandmother.

You should say about:

- True picture of maternity
- Qualities of your grandmother
- How she influences your life

My grandmother is a Goddess in the form of a woman. The sole aim of her life is service and sacrifice. Thus she deserves and claims or commands respect in our family.

My grandmother is the busiest member of the family. She is the most important wheel in the family vehicle. She is the lady who nurses and looks after children. She is a religious woman. Soon after getting up before down, she takes her bath and absorbs herself in prayer. She reads holy books and recites in a sing-song manner, while sitting before the temple that she has set up in the house. My grandmother is a great cook. She loves to prepare meals and serves delicious food to all the members of the family. She infact, acts like a machine. She is a healthy and a stout lady. She looks after every work of the house. We therefore love her very much. We all consult her in all the matters of the family. Thus, our family affairs are running smoothly. There is no difficulty before us. There is no quarrel among us.

She is very kind and considerate. She is very hard working. She never wastes a single moment of her life. Thus, our family is progressing by leaps and bounds under her tutelage. She takes care of all of us. She is not fond of showy clothes or ornaments. She is very hospitable and an ideal and pious lady.

Cue-Card 30

Describe your Friend

You should say about:

– Role of friendship

– Qualities of your friend

Man is a social animal. To lead his life, he needs friends. All friends cannot be good. But life is spend best in the company of a good and faithful friend. I have many friends, but Anoop is my best friend. I like him the most. He belongs to a noble family. His father is a doctor. His mother is a teacher in the local Government Senior Secondary School. They love me very much. I also respect them.

Anoop is my class fellow. He is my neighbour too. He has simple habits. He always speaks the truth. He is very hardworking. He considers work as worship and is very good at studies. Whenever I have any difficulty, I approach him for help. He is ever ready to help me. In reality, he really helps all the weak boys. He is a patriot and loves his country very much. He respects the elders and obeys them without hesitation. He is a good player too and a member of the hockey team. He is my true friend. I love and respect him, and he loves me a lot. In his case, it can truly be said, 'a friend in need is a friend indeed' as he is ever ready to help me when ever I need it.

Follow up Questions

1. **Most of the youngsters of these days are crazy for friendly oriented sites? Are you?**

Ans. Yes Facebook – A social networking site for joining friends according to our wishes. Each member can become friends of any of the friends in their list and can also evaluate whether their friend is trustworthy or not. It opens account of his friends on the internet. Moreover, any individual can easily get recognition name or fame in the short period of time.

2. **Is it worth to make friends online?**

Ans. It is a personal matter. For some it's worthful and for some its not, but in my opinion making friends online is not worthful because distant relationships are not successful at all.

3. **What is the difference between friend and companion?**

Ans. Friend is the trustee who will always be ready to help you and stand by you, whereas, a companion is a person who gives you company in a certain time, e.g., on trekking or a business visit.

Cue-Card 31

Describe an ideal student

You should say:

– Meaning of a student

– Work of a student

– Qualities of a student

The word, student means one who studies. Therefore, the first quality of an ideal student is that he pays special attention towards his studies. He must be hardworking, and must know that a sound mind lives in a sound body. A good and ideal student must be receptive, i.e., he should have the ability to grasp what is taught to him without any mental resistance to it. He should be adaptive, i.e., he should understand and adjust to the progressive tasks of learning. He should be honest, hardworking and curious. He must be courteous and correct, polished and polite in his conduct and behaviour. He should put all his interests towards his studies and become a notable person in his life.. Infact, everywhere, at home at college or outside, he should have the urge and desire to learn.

Follow up Questions

1. **Should we remain in touch with our teachers even after completion of our studies?**

Ans. It is indeed a good idea to be in touch with our teachers after finishing our studies. We get support, blessings and guidance from our teachers when we meet them. On the other hand, teachers also get inspired to do better by receiving love, respect and recognition from us.

2. **How is a teacher-student relationship maintained after the completion of studies?**

Ans. In most of the schools, an alumni meet is organised where old students are invited in their alma-mater for sharing their grooming personalities with their old teachers and professors. Apart from this, as we are heading towards the global world, communication is maintained with teachers and almost everyone through cell phones, email ids, etc.

Cue-Card 32

Describe an ideal teacher

You should say:

– Qualities of an ideal teacher

– Method of teaching

– As a Nation Builder

An ideal teacher is a nation builder with his morality and high ideals. With his magic touch, an ideal teacher works miracles. He teaches his student lessons not only from the text books but also from his heart. He is therefore, a missionary in teaching. His mission in life is to serve the cause of education wholeheartedly. He loves his job and enjoys popularity for his methodical teaching and sweet temper. Now and then he would tell us a joke and make us laugh. His method of teaching is very effective indeed! His lessons have both charm and spirit. His duties, however, do not end with the classroom. He reads the likes and dislikes of his pupils. His orientation regarding the career life is very clear and straight forward. One thing which makes the teacher very esteemed is that his job is not professional and corporate type, rather his job involves service to the whole mankind. He shapes the students as the ideal citizens of tomorrow. It is rightly said that the prosperity of the nation depends upon good teachers.

Follow up Questions

1. **Do you think teachers have any influence on the society?**

Ans. Yes of course. Teachers are the real builders of the societial pyramids. They are the masters and experts in their fields at such a length which make the nation proud with their deeds of learning. Moreover, their followers are also ready to adopt everything that such personalities believe.

2. **Why do youngsters hesitate in taking teaching as a profession?**

Ans. Teaching requires a lot of effort, learning and commitment to get the best out of the rest. It is also considered to be a slow growing job, where chances of earning are little less. On the other hand, nowadays, the corporate world offers many new innovative and fast growing options because of which most of the youngsters are interested to join MNCs instead of working in the public sector units.

3. **Do you like to study with a teacher having strict nature or a teacher having friendly nature?**

Ans. Teachers should be strict as well as friendly by nature. Teachers must take disciplinary action if any student tries to misbehave in the class, but if every student follows ideals and lessons of even teachers then teachers can act friendly.

Cue-Card 33

Describe an ideal citizen

You should say :

– What is special about an ideal citizen

– What are his moral Obligations and social strategies

– What are his contributions towards the country

An ideal citizen is one who liver and allows others to live. He is ready to cut short his personal freedom. He does not cry much for his rights only, but performs his duties, as well. He abides the state laws, and is loyal. He must be secular by nature, and respects all religions. He proves to be a nice neighbour who is ever to share the joys and sorrows of his neighbours. He hates bribery. He is gifted with a sense of cleanliness. He must be a regular tax payer, and respects the right of his fellow citizens and does not trespass them. He casts his vote honestly and judiciously at the time of election. Above all, he is a patriot to the backbone. He is ever prepared to sacrifice his everything for his country. An ideal citizen is a person who lives in a state and is governed by its laws in all matters. An ideal citizen is an asset to the nation.

A citizen has to carry certain duties and responsibilities. He is expected to obey the laws of his country. He must be loyal to the state. He has a great civil sense. He never wastes water, electricity, petroleum of any kind of fuel, etc. He does not spread pollution by cutting down trees or by burning wood, paper, rubber, plastic or by any other means. Hence, all these qualities, he is certainly an asset to the society.

Follow up Questions

1. **Are you an ideal citizen?**

Ans. Yes. of course, I am a true patriot of my Nation. I respect my Constitution, National Flag and National Anthem. I cherish myself with the noble ideas which answer our freedom struggle to get the freedom for the country.

2. **What are the duties of the citizens towards their nation?**

Ans. The basic priority of every citizen is to protect the sovereignty, integrity and territory of the nation from outside attack. Apart from this, every citizen should ready to achieve excellence in every field, especially on scientific and human grounds.

3. **What are the facilities given by the state to the citizens?**

Ans. A citizen enjoys several facilities. The state provides him essential services, such as transport, right of voting, electricity, hospital and schools, education for children etc.

Cue-Card 34

Describe your visit to an exhibition

You should say:

- Name of the exhibition
- Famous artist
- Artistic skills of artists

An exhibition is the mirror of a country's past, present and future's progress. It is indeed a very interesting and instructive entertainment. It is an instrument of publicity. It has a great commercial and educative value. In short, an exhibition is a great show. It is a public display of the work of art, product of industry, etc.

Last month an exhibition of Modern Indian Paintings was held at Welkon Palace. I went to see the exhibition in the company of my friends. We went there and purchased two tickets and entered the art gallery. We saw the paintings by eminent artists, fixed on the walls. The names of the artists were written in block betters. First, we saw the painting of Rabindranath Tagore, Nand Lal Bose and their disciples. Their paintings resembled the human figures in the Ajanta caves. Next, I saw the painting of Amrita Shergill. She has shown the true picture of the poor masses in India. There were many figures of Punjabi women, Sikh and little naked babies. The paintings of Satish Gujral were very much impressive. *Adam and Eve*, the *Black Road* and the Red Tomb impressed me a lot.

The paintings of Jamini Roy were very decorative.

The colours were sharp and the paintings of M.F. Hussain were very simple. The *toy house*, *sunrise,* were very fine paintings. Last of all, we saw the paintings of Thakur Singh. Really, he is a great artist. His pictures of the national and spiritual leaders appealed me the most. After seeing this fabulous exhibition, I felt that art is so lively. It took me about three hours to go round the art gallery. I returned home with sweet memories of shapes and colours. I was so much impressed by the talented Indian artists.

Follow up Questions

1. How exhibition useful for a common man?

Ans. An Exhibition is the mirror which reflects the light of culture, heritage and values of the society. It doesn't only widen the outlook of man, but also enhances the educational level of the individual. Through exhibition we come to know many new things which appear Greek to us.

2. What kind of exhibition is organized in your country.

Ans. An exhibition is the heart of culture. Basically, in my country exhibitions of artistic gallery, cosmetics, cutlery items, wardrobe settings, dressing styles, etc. are organized. But these days, private sectors organising 'Expos' for selling their products like Ratan Tata organised 'Auto-Expo' to present the new Model of car called 'NANO'.

3. **Is there any separate place meant for holding exhibitions in your city?**

Ans. Yes, in my city there is a place known an Welkom Palace which is exclusively meant for holding exhibitions.

4. **Which type of people are most fond of visiting exhibitions?**

Ans. Normally, people belonging to the high profile, educationists, lecturers, professors and elite section of the society.

Cue-Card 35

Describe Your visit to a Hill Station

You should say:

– When you visited it

– Where you visited it

– Why you visited it

A hill station is a beautiful place to visit. My uncle lives at Shimla. I received an invitation from him to visit that place during my Autumn break. On the fixed day, I boarded the Kalka Mail at 10 P.M. I reached the Kalka station at six in the morning. I then changed the train. Now I was to proceed to Shimla on a narrow guage train. On the way, the train passed many tunnels. It moved like a snake. In the beginning the journey was very thrilling but after three or four hours, it became tiresome. At last, I reached Shimla. I was received by my uncle at the railway station. The tall mountains and the dark woods presented a memorable sight. I saw many monkeys on the branches of the trees. It started drizzling before we reached home.

I stayed there for two weeks. There I visited Chotta Shimla, Lakkar Bazar, the temple of Jakku and many other places there. I also visited Kufri and had a view of snow. I enjoyed my visit a lot and brought fruits and beautiful presents from there. The beauty of the hills, the evergreen tall trees and the majestic mountains really present an exotic picturesque.

Follow up Questions

1. **Do you think 'Travelling' is the important part of education?**

Ans. Yes, travelling is an important part of education in our schools and colleges. It gives us a first hand information about things, places, persons and events. It is essential for the healthy growth of the mind.

2. **What are the advantages of tours and trips?**

Ans. Tours and trips fulfill both fun and pleasure. It doesn't only educate the student but also provide a healthy change from the mere dull, academic culture. It improves our health due to climate changes. It removes the boredom of the prosaic severity of daily life in the plains. It saves us from the grilling heat of the plains.

3. **Can you describe the mountains of a hill station?**

Ans. Mountains have a peculiar charm. The greenery, the snow, the flowers, the flora and fauna, and the springs and rivulets present a special view which is really breathtaking and marvellous. The call of very often, mountains is compelling indeed to a lover of mountains.

Cue-Card 36

Describe your visit to School/College Library

You should say:

– When do you visit it

– Why do you visit it

– What are its important parts

A library is a place where everyone can come and study by borrowing books, magazines and newspapers from there. A library is the heart of a college. Our college has a good library. I visit it almost daily during my free periods. It has about 25000 books on various subjects. It is situated in a newly constructed block known as the 'Library Block'. Our college has recently introduced the open shelf system. The books are no more kept under lock and key. They are within the reach of one's hand. The students and the members of the staff come and select the books of their own choices. There is a reading room attached to the library. Newspapers are kept on the stands. The periodicals are placed on a big centre table. The reading room is crowded through and the day. The students come there during their free period and read stories, poems and articles. It is always rewarding to spend a period or two in the reading room or the library.

Follow up Questions

1. **What do you mean by a'Library"**

Ans. A library is nothing but a collection of books, magazines and papers. Books contain knowledge and a library contains books. A library is a temple of knowledge and a room to people. It is the place where knowledge is preserved.

2. **What are the uses of libraries?**

Ans. A library spreads knowledge. It inspires students to develop a habit of reading books. Moreover, a library not only spreads knowledge, but also preserves it. It also increases our knowledge and develops our qualities.

3. **Do you think a library satisfies our knowledge?**

Ans. Yes, knowledge is both a power as well as joy. A library gives us real satisfaction and pleasure. A library is the stock house of knowledge which is useful to professional, general readers and research students. A library contains the essence of culture and hence, it should be maintained in the last possible manner.

4. **Why has every library a reading room?**

Ans. Every library has a reading room attached to it. This reading room provides atmosphere where every man wants to study the books. A reader remains in touch with the new discoveries, inventions and day to day matters of the world.

Cue-Card 37

Describe your visit to a historical place

Where did you visit it

When did you visit it

Why did you visit it

India has a large number of historical buildings which attract people from all over the world. The Taj Mahal is the most magnificent monument in India. It is called one of the Seven Wonders of the World. Last year, I went to Agra on an educational tour. We lost no time in visiting the Taj Mahal. We were highly impressed by the beautiful and majestic Taj. Its location is on the bank of the holy Yamuna. Its workmanship and the Cypress garden surrounding it, add solemnity to this wonder of the world. Then we visited the Taj at night. Luckily, it was a full moon night. We were enchanted by the beauty of the monument. It reminded us of the great emperor Shah jahan's love for his wife and his desire to immortalise his love for her. We engaged a guide. He gave us useful details about the historical background of the Taj. The next morning, we took some photographs. Then we went to Fatehpur Sikri, a walled town at a distance of about 40 kilometers (23 miles) from Agra. Then we came back to Agra and visited Sikandra and the Agra fort. Some historians have named it "The crown of the world" and Some have rightly called it is a *poem in Mahal*.

In short, it is a paradise on *earth*. The crimson rays of the son at the time of sunset enhances its beauty and glory. My joy know no bounds on seeing this wonderful building. Its memory will always remain fresh in my mind. I was reminded of the English lady who on seeing the Taj had said to her husband, "If you promise to build a monument like the Taj in my memory, I am ready to die right now."

Follow up Questions

1. What kind of dangers are the historical buildings exposed to?

Ans. The first danger to historical buildings is from *pollution, global warming and acid rain* because the gases emitted by these harmful dangers grade the surface of prominent monuments. The second danger is from the careless visitors and tourists who are fond of graffiti making which robs the beauty of the monuments. The third danger is from terrorists who have no respect for such places. The fourth danger is war and the fifth is natural calamities, such as earthquakes, lighting etc.

2. What should governments/officials do to prevent such places from pollution?

Ans. The Government should provide national security to protect the legacy of historical monuments from visitors and anti-social activists. On the other hand, individuals should behave responsibly when they visit historical places. They should not damage any part of the monuments, and maintain cleanliness of the area by throwing garbage in garbage bins only.

3. Why are historical places so important for mankind?

Ans. History acts as a bridge between the past and the present and man learns a lot about the past from these places. The historical places tell us about the special quotations of civilization, culture and architecture of these periods.

ABSTRACT

FOLLOW-UP QUERIES

This is the third part of IELTS Speaking Test which is called "Extended Discourse". It is also known as Follow up session. In other words, Follow up session means extended discussion upon the topic which already presented by the candidate in cue cards.For example, if candidate presented a cue card related to 'An Ideal Student' then in follow up session most of the queries are related to Education; Student-Teacher Relationships etc.

MOST POPULAR DISCUSSION TOPICS

Topic No. 1 – Art

1. **What are the responsibilities of museums and art gallery?**

Ans. A Museum or art gallery curators are responsible of collections for objects of artistic, scientific, historical and general interest. The emphasis of the job is on interpreting collections and making them accessible to as many people as possible. Other aspects are developing, collections, researching and cataloging items, the care and storage of objects, planning displays or exhibitions.

2. **Why are museums and art galleries created?**

Ans. India was rich in culture and heritage in the past and also in the present which has resulted in the construction of many Museums and Art Galleries. These museums and art galleries in India have preserved the ancient legacy. From these places, one can also know about the lifestyles, traditions, customs, dresses and other facts about the ancient India.

3. **What are some of the career options related to museums?**

Ans. It is possible to pursue a serious career in the museum world. One can become *Curators* by opting museum as a career. It is essentially responsible for conducting research in order to set up exhibitions at the museum. The curator and its team are responsible for designing and setting up exhibitions and also coming up with all the literatures within the gallery.

4. **What is the significance of art in our lives?**

Ans. Throughout the ages, art has played a crucial role in our lives. Art is universal and because art is everywhere, we experience it on a daily basis. From the houses, we live in (architecture) to the movies we see (theatre), to the books that we read (literature). Even in ancient culture, art has played a crucial role. In prehistoric times, cave dwellers drew on the walls of the caves to record history. In Biblical times, paintings recorded the life and death of Christ. Throughout time, art has recorded history. Most of the art is created for a specific reason or purpose, it has a way of expressing ideas and beliefs, and it can record the experiences of all people.

5. **Describe the Handicraft Industry of your country?**

Ans. India is a country of rich and diverse tradition, colours, fragrances, festivals and languages. Today, owing to the increasing handicraft manufacturing and handicraft exports, the Indian traditional handicraft culture has reached every nook and corner of the world. The legacy of Indian handicraft culture promises everything – beauty, dignity, form and style. The majestic appeal of the arts of India lies in its exclusivity and mystical tone which leaves people frenzied. The sheer versatility of the various metals and materials are used to create handcrafts and handcrafted gift items, such as wood, stone, metal, grass, paper mache, glass, cane and bamboo, textiles, clay, terracotta and ceramics, makes handcrafted items from India truly unique. Handicraft items manufactured and exported from India largely consist of vases, candle stands, Christmas ornaments, pen holders, brassware, paper mache, gift items, ceramic pots handmade paper products, etc.

6. **Describe the culture of your country?**

Ans. India's culture is like a rainbow of multiple facets which accommodates music, dance, performing arts, paintings and literature in itself and have gained recognition and fame from every corner of the world. "The cultural diversity of India gives it a distinct identity of its own which mesmerizes the entire world with its treasure and jewels of unity and harmony.

7. **What does Art teach you?**

Ans. It teaches me humility. Art definitely takes me away from reality. It also teaches me that a true artist doesn't care what other people think about his/her work. Art is an outcome of nature's beauty, a message through a man from the God itself. It opens your imagination and sometimes changes your perspectives on objects and there relativity in our surroundings. Art is a way to escape the norm and allow us the freedom to change how we perceive life.

8. **What is the importance of Art in education?**

Ans. The art instills foundational skills needed for employment, but also for life, skills like reasoning, making decisions, thinking creatively, solving problems and visualizing. (2) Those who participated in art programs are much more likely to be high academic achievers, elected to class office, participate in math and science fairs and win academic awards. Young children who participate in after-school art programs have shown a decrease in negative behaviour and increases the attention span, commitment and tolerance.

9. **What inner qualities are required on behalf of an artist?**

Ans. Artists should be patient, persistent, creative, inventive, open to new ideas and concepts, and fully committed to producing the finest art possible.

Practice Questions

1. What is the importance of Museums?
2. What is the future of art and culture?.
3. Do you think your country art and culture earn huge foreign exchange?
4. What can you do to preserve the art and culture of your country?
5. What is the correlation between art and culture?

Topic No. 2 – Teenagers

1. **Describe teenage life?**

Ans. Young people are often told, "Teenage years are the best years of your life-treasure it". Life of many youths of this new day and age involves a painful tug–of–war consisting of mixed messages, unanswerable questions, of emotions and incompatible demands from parents, teachers, friends and oneself. For youths, this period of life involves exiting the sheltered period of teenhood and reliance on others, and attaining adulthood and independence. This period in life is concomitant with many problems, as youths struggle to find answers to life, and fit themselves into the community and the society.

2. **What are the problems faced by teenagers?**

Ans. These are multiple problems with the present teenagers. The most common problems faced by teenagers on which he immediatly attention is anger management, bullies, drugs and alcohol, eating discorders, mentoring, parenting teens, out of school time, etc.

3. **Do you think teenage love is real love or just an infatuation?**

Ans. Teenage love is not real love. It is just an infatuation. Teenagers don't understand the difference between love and infatuation. I can say its only physical attraction and mental distraction.

4. **How to boost self-esteem in teenagers?**

Ans. Teenage is the most critical age in a man's life as the person is torn between adulthood and boyhood. It's a premature stage of getting adult and every aspect comes like a mystery to him. It is advisable to treat teenage brother, son or daughter as your friend and be frank with them. Do advise him/her about socializing in the best possible way in the society. Let him go where his interest makes him excel.

5. **Why do some teenagers commit suicide?**

Ans. We don't know for sure, because when teenagers die by suicide they take the answers with them. But teens who attempt suicide and survive tell us that they wanted to die to end the pain of living. They are often found experiencing a number of stresses and feel that they do not have the strength or desire to continue living. We also believe that the majority of youth who die by suicide have a mental disorder, like depression, which is often undiagnosed, untreated or both.

6. **How can schools and communities work together to prevent suicide?**

Ans. The Centres for Disease Control recommends that local mental health agencies, crisis centres, clergy, health department, medical organizations, injury prevention agencies, schools and other community members should work together to develop goals and strategies to prevent suicide.

7. **What are 'peers'? How do they influence the behaviour of teens?**

Ans. Peers are group of people who have a close but generic relationship to one another. For instance, people of a similar age group, people in the same circle of friends, people in the same class, people in the same counselling group, people in the same volunteer group, people at the same workplace, people in the same family, etc. In order for a group to be considered a "peer group", we look for one or more of these commonalities. It influences the behaviour and emotions of the teens.

8. **What is peer pressure?**

Ans. Peer pressure is a social force exerted by a group or powerful/admired individuals within a group. It is generally a pressure to conform to a social norm within any given group. Not all peer pressure is bad. Social norms are very important part of human interaction and group dynamics. Social norms are expectations that a group has of its members usually related to behaviour. Since most social norms contribute to the smooth interaction of individuals within the society, peer pressure that promotes conforming to these norms serves a positive purpose. When social norms become *deviant or harmful* or when the social norms in a group are radically different to the generally accepted social norms of a society, then we consider them to be 'bad'. When most people think of peer pressure, they are thinking of the pressure to conform to a deviant behaviour set. Things like drug use or criminal behaviour are examples of the *negative peer pressure* associated with teens.

9. **Do you think giving freedom to teenagers is spoiling their lives?**

Ans. No.... Not at All. It's a kind of experience for them. But It depends upon their age. If it is above 17, then they are capable of judging themselves. So, no worries. One shall not feel that their parents doubt him or her. And lastly, they should at least fear their parents, then their freedom will be justified.

10. **Why his/her some teenagers appear obese?**

Ans. Eating junk food or not eating a healthy diet, not enough exercise, sitting in front of a computer for long hours can cause teenage girls to get fat butts and thicker waists. Being a couch potato, is the result of drinking too much beer too often.

Practice Questions

1. Is teenage love a fantasy?
2. Do you think teenagers should do jobs, while they are still students?
3. How to earn money as a teenager?
4. What are some good hobbies as a teenager?
5. Why do teenagers suffer from low self-esteem?
6. What are the most memorable moments of your teenage time?

Topic No. 3 – Women

1. **What are some of the problems faced by the women in India?**

Ans. The problems Indian women face are same as those faced by their counterparts in other nations. Additionally, there are some unique problems in India for women.

- ✮ The Dowry System
- ✮ Desire for male progeny

Unwanted touching of women in public places – this problem is known as *Eve Teasing* in India. Ill treatment of widows -- many families blame the untimely death of a husband to the misfortune of the woman. In extreme cases, the widow is made to wear only unattractive clothing and shave her head usually in village and small towns, although this practice is on the decline.

2. **Why do Indian women wear dots on their foreheads?**

Ans. Traditionally, the dot (known as bindi, kum-kum) was the symbol of an auspicious privilege enjoyed by married Hindu women in India. The practice has now evolved to cover young girls and women of other faiths as well and has become a part of the make-up.

3. **What is the status of women in Indian society?**

Ans. The answer is a complex one – women are both abused as well as revered in the Indian society; sometimes within the same household. The Hindu religion calls for worship of womanhood, and several rituals are conducted in the honour of women. At the same time, women are denied such privileges as performing the last rites and equal share of inheritance. The conditions of divorced women widows, and unmarried working women need substantial improvement.

4. **How do the women in India spend their time?**

Ans. Indian women spend time with the family members – mostly with other female relatives. The educated women have friends they made in school or have made in their workplace. (Contrary to the old perception, a large percentage of women in India work) The Indian women also spend time with their houshold chores, raising children, watching movies and caring for families.

5. **Who is more responsive man or woman and why?**

Ans. To me both man and woman, both are responsive. Firstly, if a man earns the money and the woman works in the home front each performing his/her respective duties. Secondly, if a woman earns and the man works in home, it again balances each other's work. Hence both are responsive.... Giving the title of responsive to one among both will be injustice to one another sheer as both man and woman are responsive in each other's life as both are helpful to each other.

6. **What does woman want in a man?**

Ans. Woman wants a man should be loving, caring, handsome, attractive, financially stable and understand her. Woman lots of love and care for her and family from man. She needs a man to satisfy her perfectly in all aspects of life. She wants a man to be confident.

7. **Tell me something about women rights in your country?**

Ans. Women have equal rights as compared to men. They have right to education, job, property....etc and many other rights they can acquired in our country when she attains a age of 18 years. They acquire a right to vote, to drive and to marry as per their will......No one can force them to marry against their will.

Practice Questions

1. What are the leading causes of depression and anxiety in women today?
2. What are the roles of women as the builders of nation?
3. Why do men believe housework is a women's job?

Topic No. 4 – Internet Addiction

1. **What is an Internet Addiction?**

Ans. Internet addiction is defined as any online-related, compulsive behaviour which interferes with the normal living and causes severe stress on families, friends, loved ones, and one's work environment. Internet addiction has been called *internet dependency* and internet compulsivity. Internet addicts make the internet a priority and more important than families, friends, and work. The internet becomes the organizing principle of the addicts' lives. They are willing to sacrifice what they cherish most in order to preserve and continue their unhealthy behaviour.

2. **What causes Internet Addiction?**

Ans. Internet Addiction can be understood by comparing it to other types of addictions.

Individuals are addicted to alcohol or other drugs, for example, develop a relationship with their "chemical (s) of choice" – a relationship that takes precedence over any and all other aspects of their lives. Addicts find they need drugs merely to feel *normal.* In Internet addiction, a parallel situation exists. The Internet – Like food or drugs in other addictions – provides the "high" and addicts become dependent on this cyberspace high to feel normal. They substitute unhealthy relationships for healthy ones. They opt for temporary pleasure rather than the deeper qualities of "normal" intimate relationships. Internet addiction follows the same progressive nature of other addictions. Internet addicts struggle to control their behaviours, and experience despair over their constant failure to do so. Their loss of self-esteem grows, fueling the need to escape even further into their addictive behaviours. A sense of powerlessness pervades the lives of addicts.

3. **What are the types of Internet Addiction?**

Ans. Cybersex and Cyberporn addiction are the most common form of Internet Addictions. The widespread availability of sexual content online has given rise to a new form of sexual addiction as almost 60% of the cases of online sexual compulsivity seen result exclusively from Internet use. New problems related to online affairs have also emerged as a sub-type of Internet abuse given the widespread popularity of interactive online applications such as chat rooms and instant messaging leading to surprising new trends in divorce and marital separation. Finally addictions to eBay, online gambling, and multi-user role-playing online games are growing new forms of Internet abuse.

4. **Do men and women differ in what they become addicted to?**

Ans. Gender influences must be a underlying reason for Internet addiction. Men tend to seek out dominance and sexual fantasy online, while women seek out close friendship, romantic partners, and prefer anonymous communication in which to hide their appearance. Men are more likely to become addicted to online games, cyberporn, and online gambling, while women are more likely to become addicted to chatting, instant messaging, eBay, and online shopping. It seems to be a natural conclusion that attributes of gender played out in cyberspace parallel the stereotypes men and women have in our society.

5. **Who is most at risk for developing Internet Addiction?**

Ans. National surveys revealed that over 50% of Internet Addicts also suffered from other addictions, mainly drugs, alcohol, smoking and sex. Trends also showed that Internet Addicts suffer from emotional problems, such as *depression* and *anxiety-related disorders* and offer us the fantasy world of the Internet to psychologically escape unpleasant feelings of stressful situations. Internet addicts also suffer from relationship problems in almost 75% of the cases and use interactive online applications, such as chat rooms, instant messaging, or online games as a safe way of establishing new relationships and more confidently relating to others through the Internet.

Topic No. 5 – Time

1. **What is Time Management?**

Ans. Time management refers to the arrangement of skills, tools and techniques utilised to accomplish the specific tasks, projects and goals. This sets a wide scope of activities, which include planning, setting goals, delegation, analysis of time spent, monitoring, organizing, scheduling, and prioritising. Initially time management referred to just business or work activities, but eventually, the term broadened to include personal activities also. A time management system is a designed combination of processes, tools and techniques.

2. **How can students manage time?**

Ans. When a student learns to manage his time, he does not only learn to use his time wisely, but also understands the significance every second. He/she prioritises his/her tasks, and makes use of spare time intelligently.

3. **Why is time management so important?**

Ans. Time is the most important commodity. It never rewinds like a videotape. You can get more money but you cannot get more time. Time management is indeed a gem. Once it becomes a habit, it will be more beneficial than time – consuming.

4. **Why is time very important in our lives?**

Ans. Time is very precious and no matter what price you pay for it, you cannot buy the time which is gone. So, it is important we all value time and make right use of it. We can waste money and earn it back but time once spent cannot be earned back. So, spend the time in a righteous way.

5. **Do you always think that time is important to in all the walks of life?**

Ans. Being on time is certainly important and greatly appreciated in the professional world too…yes…. Yes, it is very important to do things on time. Time management plays a pivotal role these days in the success of any individual since if you don't do things on time then your competitors would do it and they would grow faster in life. Its imperative that you manage your time well.

6. **If life gets changed by time then why not time gets changed by life?**

Ans. Time is precious, it passes on. It never waits for anything, anybody. It does its duty, so as life changes, time moves with its own speed. Man has to move as per the time.

7. **What is the principle of Time and Management?**

Ans. The basic principle of time and management is NOW. Here N=stands for not tomorrow, O=stands for Opportunity is knocking, so take the advantage of it ,W=Stands for watch out for time gobblers.

Practice Questions

1. What is important in our life : Time, Money or Security?
2. How to start life the second time when the first time, everything goes wrong?
3. How to get yourself oriented to manage your time?
4. What is important Time or Friend?
5. If time is so precious, why do people always do time pass?
6. Time is money. Explain.
7. What would you do with your time if you are passionate about your life?

Topic No. 6 – Animals

1. **How are animals useful to mankind?**

Ans. Animals are useful to mankind in many ways. Every animal fits into the system of nature. Animals support life by serving as food for both men and plants. At the same time, they also destroy life by killing other animals or damaging crops totally. In this way, they help to keep in balance the total number of plants and animals on this earth. This vital ecosystem of the balance in nature is known as the 'Web of Life'.

2. **Why are animals called as man's best partners friends?**

Ans. Many animals have been man's best partners or friends in war or peace. Horses, elephants and even yaks were used in battlefields when other modes of transport had still not been invented. The most important function of mankind is as a provider of food. Animal domestication has solved man's most urgent need, i.e., the need of food supply on a permanent basis instead of hunting and food gathering.

3. **Describe the wildlife of your country?**

Ans. The Indian peninsula is a continent in itself rightly called as a sub-continent, whose geographical diversity has encouraged the flourishing of a whole range of wildlife with over *350 species of mammals* and *1200 species of birds* in the country. Two of India's most impressive animals, the Bengal/Indian Tiger and the Asiatic Elephant are found in most regions. These huge mammals are respected by all the animals, including the tiger. Today, most of India's wildlife finds refuge in over two hundred sanctuaries and parks around the country.

4. **Why are animals and birds getting extinct?**

Ans. Animals and birds are getting extinct because we, humans are continuously moving in on land that belong to them, destroying their homes and habitats, leaving them struggling to survive. This can end in extinction. Also, we are heartlessly poaching many animals that should be protected.

5. **Why are animals in danger?**

Ans. The animals are said to be in danger when they are at the stage of extinction. These occur due to the activities of humans like overutilising the resources of the earth. The greediness of humans beings is the many reasons behind all this. When there is massive hunting or killing of animals, the number of those animals will naturally decrease from the environment. To avoid this, we have built wildlife sanctuaries to protect the animals from extinction.

6. **What is poaching?**

Ans. Poaching can also be called *illegal hunting*, fishing, or eating of wild plants or animals contrary to the local and international conservation and wildlife management laws. Violations of hunting laws and regulations are normally punishable by the law and, collectively, such violations are known as *poaching*.

7. **Should animals be kept in cages or hunted?**

Ans. Some people claim, that is a very good idea keeping the animals in cages, especially the endangered species or hunting them. Firstly, because leaving them free, they would be a great danger, both for the human beings and other domestic animals. Some others consider that keeping the animals in cages is a bad and a cruel idea, because most of the animals are not used with the life in captivity and die or suffer. It's not a good thought that keeping the animals in captivity, they will not harm people any more. If you leave them alone, they will never attack or harm us purposely. Like us, they also have their own liver and they must live in the middle of the nature.

8. **What are Endangered Species?**

Ans. Well, Endangered species are animals or plants that are soon to die out. This means that once they become extinct, they will never be seen on this earth again. Many animals and plants become endangered or extinct each year. Recently, however the rate of these plants and animals dying out increased dramatically. It is estimated that 27,000 species become extinct each year, about 3 an hour.

9. **What are the reasons for extinction of animals?**

Ans. There are many reasons that can cause species of animals or plants to become endangered, or even extinct. First of all, the human population has exploded since the last few decades. To accommodate the oversized human population more and more, lands are taken away from these animals or plants. Animals and plants also become endangered because of the chemicals used by the people. When people use pesticides to kill insects and other pests, they are also endangering the lives of other species around them. Hunting and trading are other reasons that threaten the lives of many innocent living creatures on the Earth.

10. **Why do people poach animals?**

Ans. For thousands of years, people are killing animals or plants just for the fun of it, or for trading. Many of them do it illegally, or poaching. People kill animals for their fur, oil, body parts, and many other things in order to fatten their wallets. These things then, are them turned into fur coat, cosmetics, perfumes, oil for lamps and traditional medicines.

11. **Do you think pollution also causes species to be endangered?**

Ans. Pollution is a huge factor causing various species of animals or plants to become endangered. By dirtying our environment, we don't only hurt ourselves, but other living creatures around us. They too need a clean habitat to survive. By innocently eating our garbage they might get poisoned or choked to death. Many incidences have been reported where birds got choked or entangled in six-packs bottle holders. Fish and birds get entangled in our fishing lines and die. Toxic waste in the water system also has caused a large number of fish to die out. Water, Air and Sound Pollution in our planet has also resulted in the killing of many innocent creatures.

Practice Questions

1. What is the role of forests in maintaining the environment?
2. Why are wild animals important?
3. Why do you think people keep pets?
4. What are the advantages and disadvantages of keeping animals in the zoo?
5. What is the future of all the endangered and extinct species of plants and animals?

Topic No. 7 – Reading Books

1. **What is an E-Book?**

Ans. Basically, eBook is an online book. eBook is the book which you can read only on computer. You can download eBooks on your system and read them.... An eBook is an electronic version of a traditional print book that can be read by using a personal computer or by using an eBook reader. And eBook reader can be a software application for use on a computer.

2. **How can be reading habits be developed among children?**

Ans. Reading habits can be developed among children by providing them books of their interests. Books with pictures, motivating them to read books, telling stories and creating curiosity to know more through reading books. Children are very keen and observative to new things. Only books with pictures help them in better visualization of the characters of the book.

3. **What is the significance of reading books?**

Ans. The importance of reading books is gaining new insight to perspectives on issues that matter to the reader that helps them to have a new understanding of the world around them. Readers can apply the insight in everyday life or as a way of building upon the knowledge that already encompasses their mind and enrich their lives.

4. **Do you think reading books build self-esteem?**

Ans. By reading more books, you become better informed and more of an expert on the topics you read about. This expertise translates into higher self esteem. Since you are so well read, people look to you for answers. Your feelings about yourself can only get better.

5. **What are the advantages of reading books?**

Ans. Reading books give you a glimpse of other cultures and places, improves concentration and focus, improves your reasoning and vocabulary skills, saves money, decreases mistakes, reduces stress and boredom from your life.

6. **Are reading books the best way to improve your personality?**

Ans. Of course! Reading books are an essential habit which improves your thinking dramatically as it is an active mental process. By reading more books and exposing yourself to new and more complete information, you will also be able to come up with more creative ideas.

7. **Do you think that the reading habits in people has decreased because of computer and internet?**

Ans. Yes, without any doubt people spend most of their time online to read things. Newspapers are also available online, so they don't read the hard copy. Generally, the habit of reading books has decreased. But still those who are passionate towards reading, they are not satisfied with online stuff.

8. **Why reading habit is declining these days?**

Ans. The reading habit of people has declined to a large extent nowadays because of the mushroom growth of the television channels and internet access. People prefer to watch TV news rather than reading newspaper and people prefer to watch the television serial with their families rather than sitting and reading a book in a closed room.

9. **What should you do to improve your writing skills?**

Ans. One should read books to gain inspiration and study how other authors tackle plots and characters. You could also subscribe to a writing magazine, as they usually contain different styles of writing. Use new and tough words while writing. Read dictionaries continuously. It will be really good for improving your vocabulary.

10. **What are the disadvantages of reading books?**

Ans. They can wear out. They can become outdated and need to be updated. They can be lost. They cannot be understood in any language except for the ones they are available in. Not everyone can read, so those who are illiterate cannot use them

Practice Questions

1. Are people losing the habit of reading?
2. Do you know the art of attracting people through reading books?
3. Why do you read books?
4. Can you recommend some books for the students?
5. Have you developed the habit of reading a book before sleep?
6. Do you preserve the books you have already read?
7. Where and when do you prefer to read books?
8. How much should a child read every day?

Topic No. 8 – Media

1. **What is mass media?**

Ans. A media that reaches to a large number of people via radio, television, movies, magazines, newspapers and the internet is called the Mass Media.

2. **What are the traditional and modern means of mass media?**

Ans. Traditional mass media are newspaper, TV, Radio and the modern one is probably the internet.

3. **What are the responsibilities of the media?**

Ans. Media is the third eye of Indian Constitution. Media should be impartial and unbiased in any sense of any party. The media should present the detailed reporting of an incident. It should encourage social journalism. A wise media is that which is not spicy and impressive but always works like a watch dog. It is the responsibility of the media not to exaggerate the things.

4. **Is media good or bad?**

Ans. The media is good or bad as it all depends upon the founder and promoter of the media. The media is good when it is unbiased and bad when it projects or exaggerates news or matters.

5. **Do you think the media needs censorship?**

Ans. I think the media needs censorship on whatever they are conveying to people. Some news channels are telling fake stories and various fake news that disturb our society. Today, we are trying to remove the blind faith from our society but such an activity of the media will increase fictitiousness. The media should remember that the nation is more important than giving breaking news and increasing TRP (Television Rating Point) rates of their channels. So, I think it is necessary to censor the media for its fictitious stories.

6. **What is Media Bias?**

Ans. Media bias is a term used for those journalists and news producers who try to manipulate the stories, events and reports of the nation just to earn good TRP (Television Rating Point) rates.

7. **Is media bias or impartial?**

Ans. Media gets biased sometimes because of Yellow Journalism. This means few people try to the use the media to propagate their personal interest. One can get any news coverage by paying its price. The media is an industry that keeps many people in its pay roll. These days unhealthy competition is going between different media channels to earn their TRP ratings. Every media channel is reacting diplomatically. But on the other side of the coin the job of this organ is equally applaudable.

8. **What is yellow Journalism?**

Ans. Yellow journalism is an unethical, sensationalism, jingoism or practices by fake news media organizations or journalists favouring some person or party for their own personal interests. It is basically untrue and biased, just to create controversies or some kind of sensation to draw the attention of the public.

9. **What one wants to see in a news channel?**

Ans. Newsworthy channels are those which inform or educates us. Every news channel must adhere to these qualities, i.e. be none-biased, honest, giving the latest, wide coverage of reliable news minimum, unnecessary speculations.

10. **What is multi-media system?**

Ans. A multiimedia system is a system which combines different types of media, such as text, webPages, hyperlinks, audio, video and graphics. The use of multimedia gives the user a multifaceted visual appeal which immediately influences the masses than a single media like text.

11. **Do you think the media is more bend towards celebrities personal affairs rather than important news?**

Ans. Yes ... it is true. These days the media encashes on the personal lives of the actors and actresses. No doubt, important news are catered to us but they make the audience so curious about their details that they even don't like to watch important social and economic issues.

12. **What do you mean by TRP rating which generally comes in media conversations?**

Ans. The Television Rating Point (TRP) is a tool provided to judge the programmes which are viewed the most. This gives us an index of the choice of the people and also the popularity of a particular channel.

13. **What is the impact of media on youngsters?**

Ans. Media is known as the *fourth pillar of democracy* and it has indeed a great impact on the minds of the youngsters. The media is the medium through which we come to know about the day to day happenings and incidents of our society, country and the world. It is very easy for the media to persuade the minds of the youngsters because they are quite flexible by nature. Sensational news, romance, love, sex, fashion and unhindered access to all information also corrupts the minds of the youngsters.

Practice Questions

1. Is media playing a big role in making our younger generations go astray?
2. Do you think the media penetrates in our daily life?
3. How to become a good journalist?
4. Do you think the media is playing a vital role in the growing politics and business of your country?
5. What is the role of media in our daily life?
6. What are the responsibilities of a journalist?
7. What are the advantages and disadvantages of the media?
8. Is media a boon or a bane?
9. What is the role of media in building up of public opinion?
10. What are the differences between the Electronic media and the Print media?

Topic No. 9 – Education

1. **What is an Educational Industry?**

Ans. An educational industry consists of academic institutions, vocational, elementary and secondary schools, and companies that provide educational and training services.

2. **Is Education a Service or an Industry?**

Ans. Those were the days when education was a service to the mankind. But these days, it turns its table towards the industrial and private sector, where profit orientation is concealed behind the service orientation in the purpose of getting and giving education.

3. **Do you think Education is more important than Experience?**

Ans. Both are equally important as compared to the other. Education imparts knowledge and knowledge when implemented now and then helps in making us experienced. What we learn is the basic education. But what we earn through our education is experience. *Education is always overshadowed by experience.* A highly educated youth in front of experienced, senior citizen seems young in minds and ideas.

4. **What type of education is relevant in today's scenario for children?**

Ans. Education is meaningful only if it is based on one's choice and not compulsion. For education to be meaningful, it must be flexible, enjoyable and everlasting. There should be an impetus for students to explore, experiment and extrapolate. In today's scenario, whichever field you may choose to specialize in – the most important point is to enjoy learning and be process-oriented rather than result-oriented. It is also important to note that education does not mean memorising facts, it means questioning and exploring the facts given. Things like work experience, learning by doing (connecting learning to practical tasks), and hands-on learning can help children find out what their skills are and make them feel connected to their own education.

5. **Which education systems is the best mono or co-education?**

Ans. Co-education provides a scope of healthy atmosphere. This is absent in the single sex educational institutions. Co-education provides scope for inter assimilation of each other. As a result, acquaintance and awareness increase. Boys and girls become more liberated and become friends. Moreover, growing up together for a long time and taking part in extracurricular activities together make the students' vision and talents wider. It definitely improves one's personality and makes him/her more smart and extrovert.

Topic No. 10 – Fashion

1. **What is the importance of fashion?**

Ans. These days fashion has become indispensable. Most of the people try to update themsleves according to the latest trend. Only with the adoption of these latest trends, makes us active, smart, alert and socially acceptable.

2. **Why does fashion change with time?**

Ans. Fashion keeps changing because innovation is its inherent nature. Any innovation is called so as it is a new thought or venture in a short period of time. When a new fashion gets popular, it speeds to all parts and those who follow don't find novelty in the old fashion any longer. This is the reason why they make changes in fashion and the mass also reflects the same change in their styles. This has become on ongoing process, which keeps the fashion changing regularly.

3. **Who are trend-setters in the fashion?**

Ans. These days, film actors and daily soaps act as trend-setters in the fashion. Young boys and girls try to imitate the actors in their clothes, hairstyles and even talking and walking styles. Even their posters and poses.

4. **Do you think people spend a lot on clothes? Why?**

Ans. Its very true nowadays as most of people are brand conscious. They have to spend and wear new and fashionable clothes. They consider it as status symbol to wear fashionable clothes. However, I personally don't believe in spending a big chunk of money on clothes because to me, it is a wastage of time and money.

5. **Who are generally more fond of fashion, men or women?**

Ans. Generally, women are more inclined towards fashion because it is common to look fashionable and beautiful for women. But the trend is changing these days, and find men too getting actively involved in fashion and related products. However, I should say that females outnumber males in following fashion.

6. **Do you think clothes can change the personality of a person?**

Ans. I don't believe in this idea. No doubt, clothes can change the outward personality of a person but not the real personality. Personality is always skin-deep. Morover, I don't like to judge people with superficial aspects and secondly, such impressions can be misleading in certain situations.

Practice Questions

1. What is the importance of traditional dress?
2. Do you think old people are also inclined towards fashionable clothes?
3. What type of fashion will be popular in future according to you?
4. Are the youngsters interested in fashion?

Topic No. 11 – Shopping

1. **Do you think there is a change in the shopping style today?**

Ans. Yes, there is a tremendous change in the shopping style today. Traditionally, consumers were not brand conscious, but in contemporary times, they are buying only branded items which brought about qualitative and quantitative change in shopping.

2. **What kind of facilities are provided by the shopping centres?**

Ans. According to me, there are some basic facilities needed by the customers, like Parking, Credit Cards, Cafeteria, ATM, Calling Booths and eating facilities should be provided at the shopping centres.

3. **Where and when do you like to shop?**

Ans. I prefer to go for shopping during weekends and sometimes on Sundays. Normally, I would like to visit shopping malls, or supermarkets for shopping. Sometimes, I do like to visit retail shops too for good dealings.

4. **What precautions should be taken while shopping or buying articles?**

Ans. While shopping or buying articles, one must ensure that a shopkeeper or vendor is a supplier of the right articles, with ISI mark, changes the right prices and gives correct measurement. We must check the reputation of the manufacturers when we buy their products. Moreover, we should examine the product carefully before we pay for them to avoid any defect or dissatisfaction in the future.

5. **What do you mean by internet shopping?**

Ans. Internet these days offer everything we need. We can buy from a pen to a helicopter by using the internet. One can also buy software, books, or products that are not available in our city or country. These days internet is basically known for e-product, e-shopping e-books for education, etc.

6. **What do you know about consumerism?**

Ans. Consumerism is where producers want to promote and utilise customers at an alarming rate. It helps companies to earn more profits on increased sales and also improves the standard of living. This will ehance economical development. However, consumerism always makes people spendthrift.

7. **What kind of skills are required for shopping?**

Ans. There are many skills required for shopping. It is not as easy as it looks. We must have sufficient knowledge of the products. We must check the reputation of the manufacturers when we buy their products. Moreover, we should examine the products carefully before we go for shopping to avoid any defect or desertification in the future.

8. **What do you mean by window shopping?**

Ans. Window shopping is an activity that customers engage in watching with no intention to purchase, possibly just to pass the time between other activities or to plan for a later purchase.

Practice Questions

1. Do you think people those days go for branded shopping?
2. What are the safeguards of shopping online?
3. What are the advantages and disadvantages of credit cards?

Topic No. 12 – Computer Technology

1. **What is computer and how does it help you?**

Ans. A computer is a machine which can take instructions, and perform computations based on those instructions. It is the ability to take instructions – often known as *programs* in the parlance of computers, and execute them, that distinguishes a computer from a mechanical calculator. The computer is one of the most powerful innovations in human history. With the use of computers, people are suddenly able to perform a staggering amount of computations at dazzling speeds. Information can be crunched, organized, and displayed with the blink of an eye.

2. **What do you mean by computer hacking?**

Ans. Computer hacking is the practice of modifying computer hardware and software to accomplish a goal outside the creator's original purpose. People who engage in computer hacking activities are often called *hackers*.

3. **Do you think computer hacking is good or bad?**

Ans. Computer hacking is good as some corporations actually employ computer hackers as part of their technical support staff. These individuals use their skills to find flaws in the company's security system, so that they can be repaired quickly. In many cases, this type of computer hacking helps prevent identity theft and other serious computer-related crimes.

Computer hacking can also lead to other constructive technological developments. But in comparison to those, who develop an interest in computer hacking out of simple intellectual curiosity, some hackers have less noble motives. Hackers who are out to steal personal information, change a corporation's financial data, break security codes to gain unauthorised network access, or conduct other destructive activities are sometimes called 'crackers.' This type of computer hacking can earn you a trip to a federal prison for up to 20 years.

4. **What is hardware and software in computers?**

Ans. Hardware refers to objects that you can actually touch like disks, disk drives, display screens, keyboards, printers, boards and chips. In contrast, software is untouchable.

Software exists as ideas, concepts and symbols, but it has no substance.

Books provide a useful analogy. The pages and the ink are the hardware, while the words, sentences, paragraphs and the overall meaning are the software. A computer without software is like a book full of blank pages. *You need software to make the computer useful, just as you need words to make a book meaningful.*

5. **What are cyber crimes?**

Ans. Cyber crime encompasses any criminal act dealing with computers and networks (called hacking). Additionally, *cyber crime also includes traditional crimes conducted through the Internet.* For example: telemarketing and Internet fraud identity theft, and credit card account thefts are considered to be cyber crimes when the illegal activities are committed through the use of a computer and the Internet.

Topic No. 13 – Colour

1. **How does colour influence our lives?**

Ans. Colour plays an important role in our lives whether we realize it or not. It has the ability to influence our feelings and emotions in a way that few other mediums can. It can control our moods and thoughts. Colour has the ability to make us feel happy, depressed, excited, relaxed, hungry or creative.

2. **Describe your dream coloured house?**

Ans. My drema coloured house consists of warm and cool colours. Warm colours work great for areas of the house, where my family and friends gather regularly. Yellow is said to promote harmony so it would be a good colour for a kitchen. The sun, sand, desert and rocks are warm things, so if I want to bring a feeling of warmth to a room, then bright colours would be a good choice. A room that is located in a shadier area and has a cool temperature can be made to feel warmer with yellow, orange and red. Cool colours, such as lavender, blue and green would work in areas where I want to relax like the den, bedroom and bathroom. Blue is calming and so it's a good colour for stress relief.

3. **What does black colour signify?**

Ans. Black is the colour of authority and power. It is popular in fashion because it makes people appear thinner. It is also stylish and timeless. Black also implies submission. Priests wear black to signify submission to God. Some fashion experts say a woman wearing black is to signify submission to men. Black outfits can also be overpowering, or make the wearer seem aloof or evil. Villains often wear black.

4. **What does red colour signify?**

Ans. The most emotionally intense colour, red stimulates a faster heartbeat and is often breathtaking. It is also the colour of love. Red clothing gets noticed and makes the wearer appear heavier. Since it is an extreme colour, red clothing might not help people in negotiations or confrontations. Red cars are popular targets for thieves. In decorating, red is usually used as an accent. Decorators say that red furniture should be perfect, since it will attract attention.

5. **What does yellow colour signify?**

Ans. Cheerful sunny yellow is an attention-getter. While it is considered an optimistic colour, people lose their temper more often in yellow rooms and babies cry more when they see yellow colour. It is the most difficult colour for the eye to take in, so it can be overpowering if overused. Yellow enhances concentration, hence, it is used for legal pads. It also speeds metabolism.

6. **What does blue colour signify?**

Ans. It is the colour of the sky and the ocean blue is one of the most popular colours. It causes the opposite reaction as red. Peaceful, tranquil blue causes the body to produce calming chemicals, so it is often used in bedrooms. Blue can also be cold and depressing. Fashion consultants recommend wearing blue to job interviews because it symbolizes loyalty. People are more productive in blue rooms. Studies show weightlifters are able to handle heavier weights in blue gyms.

7. **Do you think that the colour of clothing you wear reflects your personality?**

Ans. Yes, its very true. Clothes really exhibit your personality. When I was shy and an introvert, I wore dark, drab clothing. I really didn't want to draw attention to myself. When I finally 'blossomed', I found myself selecting clothing in red and bright yellow. I simply 'felt' more vibrant and therefore, my clothing exhibited that.

8. **Is there any festival of colours that is celebrated in your country?**

Ans. Yes, Holi demands a big time planning. Buckets and barrels of strongly coloured water have to be concocted and water balloons filled to greet friends and neighbours. The gala time starts in the morning itself. People go around smearing one another with *gulal* (coloured powder) and coloured water. Children shoot jets of water from their *pichkaris*, screaming gleefully. A lot of people spend the day alternating between getting drenched and coloured, and consuming *thandai* (a marijuana-based drink) in large quantities as the day progresses. Singing and dancing to the beat of *dholaks* (drums) completes the picture.

Practice Questions

1. How have colours powerful effects on your mood?
2. Why do some people like to wear dark colours?
3. What is the best colour outfit for an average coloured person?

4. How do colours reflect our inner character?
5. Do colours have religious importance?
6. Why do all the people consider fair colour of the human skin as a sign of beauty?

Topic No. 14 – Movies

1. **Why do movies release on Friday?**

Ans. The reason for the release of movies on Friday is due to the import of culture from the foreign lands as Indian movies follow the Hollywood culture. Indian movies follow the trend set by the Hollywood movies. In the earlier days, movies were released on Friday Night all over the world, and this trend has been carried on till now. Moreover, One simple reason would be the start of weekend.

2. **Why are Animation Movies running so popular all over the world?**

Ans. Animation Movies take you to the world of creativity. It is popular because people appreciate exploring the unexplored and as we always seek for something fresh and new, animated movies are targeted to fulfill these demands.

3. **How do movies affect children?**

Ans. Movies have a great and appreciable impression on the minds of children. It imbibes and adopts many styles of dressing, talking, walking, etc. by watching them. These impressions may either be good or dangerous for children depending on the type of movie.

4. **Do you think old movies were better than the present day movies?**

Ans. The present day movies come nowhere, near the old movies, when it comes to standards. May be owing to technological advancements and gadgets, the present movies are not so dazzling and opulent. But as the common saying 'Old is gold'. Same applies to these movies also.

5. **Does movies promote violence?**

Ans. Yes, some movies promote violence. Children's greatest exposure to violence comes from television and movies. Movies spread violence stunts hitting, kicking, stabbings, shootings, etc. has a very negative impact on the children's minds.

6. **What do you think about Bollywood as compared to Hollywood?**

Ans. Of course, Hollywood is much better than Bollywood because in Hollywood, we can find a large variety of movies but in bollywood, repetition is there in every film love, romance and family melodrama are the only three themes that Bollywood mainly deals with. Moreover, Hollywood directors are pretty bold in their movie making and in Bollywood we are pretty concerned about the movies we should show to our audience. Hollywood movies are very high budgeted movies based on missions or meaningful stories in one or two hours duration, but Bollywood movies are music, lyrics that lasted for 2 to 3 hrs.

7. **Can you watch Bollywood movies with your families?**

Ans. Nowadays Bollywood movies are heading towards nudeness in normal scenes also. With all those bold and kissing scenes, which have sort of become part of the script of almost every hindi movie today, it is really very difficult to watch such movies with family. The kind of clothes the present day actresses wear, it's not possible to watch Bollywood movies with your family. Really by aping Hollywood, Bollywood is sadly losing its identity.

8. **Are Movies a Popular source of entertainment?**

Ans. Yes, Movies are definitely one of the most popular source of entertainment. Indian Bollywood industry is the largest producer of films in Asia or rather, the world. It provides revenue and employment to millions of people directly and indirectly. According to the taste of the common man, all sorts of movies like stunts, social, romance, dance, fiction, filmy melodrama, etc. produced. People worship film stars like Amitabh Bachchan, Sharukh Khan, etc., give them the title of God.

9. **What kind of films are popular with younger generation?**

Ans. These days youngsters like to lead a fast life like a walk on the razor's edge. They are fond of *speed* and *adventure*. Hence, Action Movies with stunning feats are adopted by the youngsters especially boys. However, *comedy and action films* are the talk of the town among the youngsters.

Practice Questions

1. Do you think that pron movies should be banned as it is polluting the human society?
2. How do movies affect your society?
3. Which films do you like the most? Old or the New Ones.
4. Do movies influence human behaviour?
5. What kind of movies will be popular in future according to you?
6. Do you like to watch movies do your prefer movies in the or cinema hall?
7. How often do you prefer to watch movies?
8. With whom do you prefer to watch movies?
9. Is going to cinema as popular as it was?
10. Has technology made difference to the quality of films?

Topic No. 15 – Music

1. **Which is more popular in your country? Indian Classical Music or Western Music?**

Ans. Both have their own admirers. There is nothing like more or less. If you are young, you will be surrounded by youth and all have western choice, but if you are an elderly person, then you may have a classical choice. But in the modern era, Western music is in cities as well as in villages. Times have changed, with commercialization, globalization and modern entertainment channels and avenues. Even the older orthodox generation docs not hesitate to shake a leg to the beat of the western music. But remember one thing, music, in whatever form, knows no boundaries or cultures. *Music is the language of the soul.*

2. **Do you think our emotions and feelings are influenced by music?**

Ans. Our emotions and thoughts get completely altered and influenced by music. Music influences our emotions and behaviour to a great degree. It relaxes and energises us. It can make us sad, or happy.

3. **Is there any difference between slow and fast music?**

Ans. Slow music calms us down. Ballads, some forms of classical music, Indian sem-classical music, like Bhajans and Ghazals as well as meditation music create a peaceful atmosphere that is good for relaxing after a busy day or for a romantic dinner. For most people, slow music is de-stressing. It allows them to sit down and relax, as compare to other, faster music such as Rock, Jazz, Pop, etc.. Heavy metal and dance music tend to uplift us. It energises us, and awakens us in the real sense, making us feel full of life.

4. **What do you understand by techno music?**

Ans. Techno Music is produced using computers and almost constitute and escape into an alternate virtual world. The music is reminiscent and amalgamation of sci-fi, technology and the futuristic world that we can imagine only.

5. **Why do Rock, Pop, Dance and Rap music add flavour to social gatherings and parties?**

Ans. Rock, pop, Dance and rap music are also often played at parties, when large groups of people gather together. This is the music of socialising and being together. Most Rock. Pop and Rap songs also do not involve special efforts for listening to and are also suitable for parties. Dance music is light and yet fast. It fills us with energy and relaxes us, but it is not complicated by intellectual overtones. So it allows us to live up and unwind without having to think or listen very seriously. For this reason, it is very popular at parties.

6. **Does new remix song hurt music lovers?**

Ans. Remix is nothing but a old song in a new package. It must not hurt a music lover but it does hurt if it is picturised in vulgar way like the latest Hindi Pop song, kanta laga or the essence of the song has not been maintained. As far as music lovers are concerned, there is a generation gap, plus they don't find remix video tasteful too. Hence, it does quite irritate them.

7. **What is the significance of music in life?**

Ans. No music no life. Music makes our life peaceful and comfortable. Music plays a vital role in ones life. It has got a soothing effect. It can bring person out of depression also. It is proved that with music therapy many of the diseases can be cured. It makes me relax. The light Classical, instrumental old songs souls up our energy level and happiness, after listening to music for half an hour daily in the evening. Music is the best way to express your emotions and brings out a lot of your feelings. Its cheers our lives.

8. **Do you think with the advancement of science and technology, the music tastes of people become sci-fi?**

Ans. Technology has a great learning on the kinds of music. As new technology is developed, new music and musical instruments appear before the composers and people. Since human nature always aspire to go, learn new things, new music, etc., if it has a sound footing, it often gets acceptability. All this has a strong effect on the current musical compositions and tastes.

9. **How important is it for a country to have national music?**

Ans. The National Music in the form of a National Song gives us a national indentity, recognition and strength. It makes us feel as a true patriot and nationalist. It also create a sense of belongingness and responsibility on the behalf of every citizen. It also differentiates us from the alien citizens. It is a national legacy which we bequeathed from our forefathers after the long struggle of freedom. So, it is our moral duty to preserve, protect and pass it on over to the coming generations.

Practice Questions

1. Which type of music is more popular amongst the youngsters these days?
2. What does music mean to you? How is it important in your life?
3. Do you think music can cure an ill person?
4. What is the difference between folk and rock music?
5. What are the various music genres?
6. Is it true that music has healing power?

7. What are the healing energies of music?
8. How does music affect our society?
9. What kind of music affects our society?
10. What factors influence a person's choice of music?

Topic No. 16 – Health

1. **Can you give some tips for good health?**

Ans. One should follow these certain health tips like eat healthy and balanced nutritious food like salads, green vegetables, fruits and juices, reduce the oil intake in your diet, eat fresh fruits and vegetables, avoid drugs, alcohol and oils, drink 10-12 glasses of water daily, do yoga and fast walk for 30 minutes in morning as well as in the evening.

2. **What is health?**

Ans. When a person does not suffer from any disease, either mentally or physically, then we say, he is healthy. Health is a disease free condition. It is the state when a person is free from mental, physical, social and spiritual illnesses. He is able to manage all the things in a proper way.

3. **Do you think hygiene is associated with health?**

Ans. Hygiene refers to practices associated with ensuring good health and cleanliness. In medical context, the term 'hygiene' refers to the maintenance of health and healthy living.

4. **"Health is wealth" Do you agree with this statement?**

Ans. I agree with this statement because you can earn money again in future, but you cannot get your health back. So when money is lost, something is lost but if health is lost then everything is lost. In life, money may come and go, but health once gone never come back.

5. **What should you do to remain healthy?**

Ans. Health is the word used to describe how your body feels. Being healthy is important because it makes you feel good and live longer. I am healthy. To maintain good health, one should be eating the right food and do the right exercise as well as work hard in whichever field one wishes to. One should take medicine only when one is very ill not otherwise.

6. **Are we neglecting our health and inviting health culprits through the course of our modern way of living?**

Ans. Yes, it is true to some extent. Change in the lifestyle is one of the culprits to invite various health problems. Like, overusage of cellphones, taking more junk food, improper sex, sitting too much before computer, and also health habits like oversmoking, tatoos on skin and also overstress – all leads to ill health.

7. **Does mental health affect our physical health?**

Ans. Certainly mental health plays signifieant role in physical fitness and vice versa. If you are disturbed, stressed, in tension or in some other undesirable state, then it really affects the physical health by raising the blood pressure and the body temperature too. It also affects the food appetite which in turn results in low blood sugar and decreases the immune system.

8. **Can you suggest some health tips for our daily routine?**

Ans. In our daily routine, one must follow certain health tips like answer the phone by the left ear, do not have huge meals after 5pm, reduce the amount of oily food, we consume and drink more water in the morning but less at night.

Practice Questions

1. Which is more important? Mental Health or Physical Health?
2. In what way a good mental health is necessary?
3. How can you maintain your health?
4. What is a balanced diet for good health?
5. Do you think watching television is harmful for health?
6. How is exercise helpful to retain fitness?
7. How can health awareness be brought about among people?
8. How do medical and health care aids made available to all sections of the society?

Topic No. 17 – Games & Sports

1. **What are the basic utilities of sports and games?**

Ans. The basic utility of games is undoubtedly to help us maintain our body in keeping beautiful and healthy. This applies to all of us. All children it a for example, with delicate and fragile body frames should be encouraged, and if necessary, even forced to play games. Minor ailments like cough, headaches and fevers remain at a distance from sportsmen. Sports provide a systematic and regular exercise in a pleasing way and provide enjoyment together with sufficient physical strain.

2. **Do you think sports teach us discipline?**

Ans. Sports also play a vital role in teaching discipline among the players. A Sportsman, while at the field has always to act according to the rules of the game, with set norms of discipline of the game. This inculcates in the individual a sense of working in accordance to rules and regulations, whether he be at home, at the games field or at his office. Thus, this working as per rules gets translated into all spheres of life of the sportsman, with ease and convenience.

3. **What are the attributes of a true sportsman?**

Ans. A sportsman in the games field develops a sense of selflessness and a fellow feeling. Every sportsman imbibes his acceptance with a smile and the mistakes and drawbacks of other players of his team. Instead of fighting or abusing, a co-player for a mistake he might have made, a sportsman accepts mistakes of others and forgives them all, as he would understand and justify his own mistakes. This makes a sportsman very accommodating and considerate. Another important value imbibed in a sportsman is the sense of teamspirit which is an essential concomitant for success in later life.

4. **What are the disadvantages of playing sports and games?**

Ans. We have a lot in praise for sports but, that does not mean that sports are without any disadvantages. It has often been seen that children who are seriously interested in sports get away from studies and even from other extracurricular activities of their schools or colleges. This makes them develop into singular personality instead of towering rounded personalities.

5. **Do you think games and sports are valuable forms of education?**

Ans. Education will remain incomplete without physical training and exercise. 'All work and no play makes Jack a dull boy' is a famous saying. After studies some kind of physical exercise, games and sports are necessary that refreshes the body and mind and provide recreation. It provides us physical fitness, courage, endurance, cooperation and teamspirit. The players are more disciplined and fit than others. Sports and games along with education prepare us to stand up and face the challenges of life.

6. **Do you think these days cricket is a Game or Business?**

Ans. As far as international cricket is concerned, it is still a game, but for ICL or IPL, it is a business and nothing else other than that. The game will lose its mortality as well as its geniuses as players are reduced to disco dancers with flashy dresses flaunting all around the world, ODI Limited, Test cricket T20 Limited ODIs and now IPL and ICL will be even more mocking in terms of skills and capabilities of the cricketers. A day is not far when the footballers and other sportspersons too will be sold like lifeless products. The business tycoons are utilising the game to generate revenue from them and ultimately, the game will end in mere amusement rather than a game.

7. **Why does media hype the cricket more than any other sports in your country?**

Ans. Indians are only crazy about the game of cricket more than any other sports played in the country. Other Olympics sports like shooting, boxing and athletic sports came into light with some medals which were without money. So in cricket of there is a lot money, glamour, cheer girls, entertainment, music, passion and controversies involved. Everything is at the one platform. No other sports have all these colours in it. That's why media hypes the cricket more than any other sports.

8. **Do people in your country love to play games and sports?**

Ans. People of India are mad for cricket. As far as other sports are concerned, like the successes achieved by various Indian players in Beijing Olympics, particularly the youngsters are getting drawn towards sports.

Practice Questions

1. Do sports build your character?
2. Which is your favourite sport?
3. Which game is quite popular in your city?
4. Do you agree games have equal contributions in development?
5. What is the difference between games and sports?
6. What are the older sports /games of your country?
7. With whom do you play games?
8. Do men and women play different types of sports in your country?
9. Can sports be dangerous?
10. What are the benefits of sports and games?
11. What games did you like to watch on TV ten years ago?

Topic No. 18 – Friend

1. **Can you define the meaning of a true friend?**

Ans. A Friend denotes a companion. A friend is a person whom you can trust and share your feelings. In my opinion, a friend is that person who will be with you forever. A friend is a tender shoulder on which you softly cry. It is a well to pour your troubles down and raise your spirits high. Basically, Friendship is one soul inhabiting in two bodies.

2. **What is friendship according to your own opinion?**

Ans. Actually, friends are those who share with you, comfort at the time of need, helps you cross obstacles, cooperate with you all your way, guide you when you are wrong and like you the way you are.

3. **What does a friend expect most from his/her friend?**

Ans. A friend expects from the other friend the same that he is willing to contribute. Not much should be expected. Expectations when not met serve a serious blow to your soul. A good and sound counsel, a helpful, caring and keep in touch always, truth love and affection should be expected only form a friend. Moreover, a friend can expect from his/her friends about mental, emotional, and every type of support as well.

4. **Do you make friends before you need them?**

Ans. If we are making friends in need, then it is a business, not a friendship. Then it will be self-comfort not selfless friendship.

5. **What is the importance of friends in your life?**

Ans. Friendship is a blessing and a friend is the channel through whom we get emotional, spiritual, and sometimes, even physical blessings. Friends cheer us when we're sad or depressed. Friends often challenge us to attain our original limits with encouragement when we allow ourselves not to go beyond our reasonable boundaries. Friends motivate us when we're ready to give in, and they can provide for us when life falls apart. Friends are there when all is well, and we want someone with whom to share life's pleasant and memorable moments. We often just want them around, to have a good time, to laugh, to act silly, and to enjoy some mutually liked activity.

6. **Do you think friends are troubleshooters?**

Ans. Friends are the only source of our brave hearts. If we don't have any friends, we will never be able to come out when there is a trouble. But when we have friends with us, we face all the problems bravely. We may not be brave but friendship gives courage to our mind and body. Friends save us from every situation. Friends help us to escape from big troubles. They always come front to solve the problems. Friendship never knows to run away during problems. A good friend stays when there is a problem and goes after the problem is solved.

7. **What is the difference between a best friend, close friend, and good friend?**

Ans. Your best friend is your first priority for telling personal things, sharing adventures, and serving/giving. A close friend is a friend you trust, who knows you very well, but not as well as your best friend. A good friend is loyal and trustworthy, but he/she is not your first priority. He/She is always there when you need him/her (and vice-versa) but he/she doesn't necessarily share most of your secrets and experiences.

8. **How to help and support a friend in any hardship?**

Ans. First of all, let him/her believe that you trust him/her completely. Be open to talks. Do small things to cheer him/her up for the moment. If your friend seems to be getting worse and worse, talk to him/her about something/some one pleasant, but don't offer advice when he/she. Ask what is wrong, if he or she doesn't tell you, let it be. And lastly be a good listener. Then I think you can support your friend in any hardship.

9. **What things must be kept in mind while choosing friends?**

Ans. The choice of friends should be made vey wisely. The choice of your friends can or mar your career. 'Acquaintance with many, familiarity with a few, friendship with one and enmity with none' should be our guiding principle, while making the choice. Unequal friendship seldom lasts long. Friends should normally be almost of equal age in social status and temperament.

10. **How are your friends important to you?**

Ans. My life begins and ends with my friends. All my friends are very important to me. We are a group of five friends and we cannot pass a week without meeting one another. We share one another's joy and sorrows and constantly try to help and improve one another.

Practice Questions

1. Should we have a best friend or all friends should be considered equal?
2. How to recognize a true friend?
3. Is it worth to make friends online?
4. Is it wise to tell all secrets to the best friend?
5. What will be your reaction when someone close to you gives a bad opinion about your best friend?
6. Do you think that life has any meaning without friends?
7. How to help your friend who is suffering from depression?
8. What kind of work or studies your friends do?
9. Why does friendship break?
10. How do people choose their friends?
11. What kind of work or studies your friends do?
12. How often do you meet your friends?

Topic No. 19 – Food

1. **Why is 'Junk-Food' is harmful for health?**

Ans. Junk food is a slang used for foods with *limited nutritional value*. To put it simply, foods high in salt, sugar, fat, or calories and low nutrient content can be termed as junk food. Salted snack foods, candy, gum, desserts, fried fast food and carbonated beverages are some of the major junk foods. Junk food harms the system with empty calories. It has no proteins and vitamins.

2. **Which type of food is healthy...?**

Ans. Low fat and low calorie food are good for health. Always use less fat/oil while cooking. Healthy food includes greens, fruits and salads in our meals. Also eat plenty of dals, pulses, sprouts and low fat curds. Healthy and nutritious food are very important for maintaining a good health. Healthy food involves regular and timely food, juices, nuts, snacks and much more.

3. **What are the advantages and disadvantages of eating non-vegetarian?**

Ans. Non-vegetarian food is more tasty and less bulky unlike cereals.They are rich in proteins, such as eggs, fish, meat, etc. One should take less quantities and more protein and fats for easy body building if combined with exercise. The basic disadvantages of non-vegetarian are low fiber, less anti-oxidants, etc that causes intestinal cancer, low energy, constipation problems, etc. Vegetables may not be very tasty as the non-vegetarian but have a good food fiber, more anti-oxidants to fight many diseases.

4. **Why do Indains offer food to the Lord or God before eating it?**

Ans. Indians make a offering of food to the Lord(God) and later partake of it as prasada, a holy gift from the Lord. In our daily ritualistic worship too, we offer food to the Lord. The Lord is omnipotent and omniscient. Man is a part, while the Lord is the totality. All that we do is by his strength and knowledge alone. We acknowledge this through the act of offering food to him and this is exemplified by the Hindu words 'tera tujko arpan.'

5. **Do you think food is the part of the culture?**

Ans. Yes, food reflects a culture. It's natural for tourists to feast on the local flavour. It helps one to comprehend to locate in its totality. Depending on the climatic and environmental conditions the local cuisine is determined. For example Punjabi cuisines are identified with their special blend of vegetables like *sarso ka saag and makke ki roti*.

6. **What is the influence of modern cuisines on Indian cuisines?**

Ans. Today Indian cuisines are no more limited to the traditional Indian cuisines. The influence of westernization is prominent in the modern Indian platter as well. Food items like breads, pastas, noodles, cakes, pizzas and others such foods which were once unknown to this section of world, features prominently in the Indian kitchens today. The modern Indian cuisines pack in the traditional cuisines of India as well cuisines from other parts of the world. Over the years, newer and newer methods of cooking from different parts of the world have influenced the Indian cuisine. Vegetables like broccoli and black pepper and fruits like cherries and strawberries which were unheard of in the ancient Indian kitchens are very much used today in Indian preparations.

7. **What were the food habits of your country in the past?**

Ans. People in ancient India subsisted on food that was conveniently available from

Nature. The nomads preferred fruits, fist, wild berries and meat as their main food. With the arrival of civilization, the Indians took up agriculture as their occupation, and used grains, pulses and other agricultural products as their main food items. Most of the ancient people consume rice as their staple food. Other ancient Indian food included meat, vegetables, fruits and cooked lentils. Apart from rice and vegetables, the ancient Indians also preferred wheat products as their staple food. They made breads or 'chapattis' from wheat.

8. **What kind of food items are quite popular in your country?**

Ans. The influence of westernization is prominent in the modern Indian platter as well. Food items like breads, pastas, noodles, cakes, pizzas and others such foods which were once unknown to this section of world, features prominently in the Indian kitchens today.

9. **Does fast food make our health weak?**

Ans. Most of the fast foods have high fat content. It contains harmful salts/preservatives. This leads to obesity and could lead to many other diseases. Fast food is full of calories. If you are checking your weight regularly and are health conscious then it is better to avoid it.

10. **Does food of your country has any influence on religion?**

Ans. One of the main influences on Indian cuisine is the Hindu religion. In this religion, there is much emphasis on vegetables because many Hindus are vegetarians for ethical reasons. Over the years, Indians have used a vast range of different vegetables like spinach, tomatoes, cauliflower, potatoes and green beans to make different vegetarian dishes. Some other popular Indian vegetables include eggplant, okra, cluster beans, beetroot, cucumber and white radish. For example, Brahmins (one of the highest caste), in the Hindu religion, are strict vegetarians. They do not eat either fish or eggs. In addition to all this, most of the Hindu people, as far as I know, don't eat beef. Cows are considered sacred in India and are worshipped by the Hindus. Pork is also not eaten much because pigs in India are not raised in food environments, so eating pork can lead to different types of diseases. Most of people in my town do not eat pork.

Practice Questions

1. Which food do you like the most, Junk Food or Home-made?
2. Is there any relation between food and culture?
3. What kind of food do you enjoy eating?
4. What are some kinds of foods you never eat?
5. Do you like cooking?

6. What are nutritious and hygienic food?
7. Which type of food will be more popular in future?
8. Do you think people should be careful about what they eat?
9. Which is the most important meal of the day for you?

Topic No. 20 – Fairs and Festivals

1. **Why are fairs and festivals celebrated?**

Ans. Fairs and festivals are as old as mankind, arising from the innate desire to congregate and divert from the humdrum routine of life. They provide as index to the cultural, social and domestic life of people. Many among them are based on legends and aim at propitiating deities and persons believed to be blessed with supernatural powers, and invoking them for the grant of desires and for warding off troubles and curing aliments.

2. **What is the nature of festivals in your country?**

Ans. Festivals all of socio-religious nature which provide an atmosphere of devotion and enjoyment. Some festivals mark the seasonal changes and some are local in character and are associated with some place, saint or pir. The fairs and festivals attracting large gatherings are taken advantage of by the Government, religious and social organizations, and business firms, for doing publicity.

3. **Which is the famous festival of your hometown? Do people of your religion show same enthusiasm to other religious festival as to their own religion?**

Ans. Gurpurbs are the largest religious festivals of the Sikhs which are celebrated with great devotion and love for the Gurus. A large number of Hindus also participate in these celebrations. Big diwans are held on the birthdays of Guru Nanak Dev and Guru Gobind Singh and on the martyrdom days of Guru Arjan DEV and Guru Teg Bahadur. The Gurpurb of Guru Ravi Dass is also celebrated in February, with great enthusiasm. People also show great enthusiasm in celebrating the religious festivals of *Shivratri, Holi, Janam Ashtami, Rakhi,Dussehra, Diwali, Tikka, Ram Navami, Nirjala – Ekadashi,* etc. The seasonal festival of *Lorhi, Maghi, Basant Panchami* and *Baisakhi* are also celebrated with a good deal of fan-fare.

4. **Can you define festival, how is it celebrated, why is it celebrated?**

Ans. A festival is an occasion which you enjoy with fun and fiesta. It is an occasion to bring a change in the monotony of life. A festival takes you to meet friends and relatives, to eat, meet and greet. Traditions have set norms to celebrate them. It can be rearranged according to your own ideas of renovations.

5. **What are the benefits of festival?**

Ans. The festivals are just not for the holidays. Every festival has its own meaning. Some of the benefits of festivals, are stress-relieving from a hectic work season gathering of family members and friends, cultural exchange, etc.

6. **Why are performing rituals during festivals very important?**

Ans. Rituals are performed with utmost care to provide a very asthetic and spiritual experience during festivals. These rituals for Indian festivals have been followed for past several centuries with the same respect that was used several hundreds of years ago. Every Indian festival has different rituals and prayers that are followed. Every day of weekday has a different story (see Hindu fasts) and different reason behind having these seven days. Apart from just Hindu festivals, there are also several Muslim festivals also that follow rituals of their own. *Azzan* and is performed when a child is born, or after the new-born baby is given its first bath. These rituals are followed, and prayers are offered to God. This process is followed so that the first name that the child hears is that of the God.

7. **What sort of message is given by festivals?**

Ans. Festivals bring joy and happiness in our lives. If we celebrate all the festivals alike, we can spread the message of joy, happiness, brotherhood and humanity among one another and live as one family or as one community.

8. **What consists of celebration of festivals?**

Ans. Each celebration centres around the rituals of prayer, seeking blessings, exchanging goodwill, decorating houses, wearing new clothes, music, dance and feasting. In India, every region and every religion has something to celebrate. The festivals reflect the vigour and lifestyle of its people. Vibrant colours, music and festivity make the country come alive throughout the year.

9. **Do you think festivals are celebrated to mark the changes in the season?**

Ans. Festivals are also celebrated to mark changes in the season, such as the advent of spring or the beginning of a rainy season. One can find traces of religion as well as magic in these attempts to seek nature's magnificence. Some of the seasonal festivals include the *Baisakh*i in Punjab, *Uthran* in Gujarat and *Bihu* in Assam.

Practice Questions:

1. What is the relation between seasons and festivals?
2. Do you like to celebrate festivals with your friends or with your family?
3. Do you think festivals also change with time?
4. Is it true to say village people celebrate festivals more enthusiastically as compared to urban people?

Topic No. 21 – Family

1. **Do you think to ingrain the 'importance of family' among your children?**

Ans. Yes, it is essential to ingrain the importance of family among your children. They need to know that friends will come and go, but family is the one constant they will have in life. As a parent, it is your job to foster the bond between siblings, as well as between each parent and the child. This is especially important in a single – child family. If it's feasible, expose these children to as much time as possible with extended family members, preferably cousins, who are similar in age to them. There are many other ways to help your child realize the family is of utmost importance. This understanding will remain with them as they grow up, marry, and embark on parenthood themselves.

2. **What are the best ways for a family to spend time together?**

Ans. I believe one of the best ways for a family to spend time together is to go out into nature. This is an amazing way to commune with each other and our surroundings. We live in such a hectic, world where we're constantly being bombarded with the media from all directions. The solitude and peacefulness of nature fosters family togetherness and makes memories that will bolster children's sense of self-confidence throughout their lives.

3. **Why is eating meals together a good way to communicate with your family?**

Ans. It's almost a cliché these days to emphasize the importance of eating meals together around the table, not in front of the television or watching sports. While you are sitting there as a family, ask your children a great deal of questions about their day to day activities, not in an accusatory, meddling fashion, but in a way that shows interest and concern for their daily activities. Meals should be a peaceful, joyous time and it's important to create an atmosphere that's conducive to good communications.

4. **Do you think a joint family is a happy family?**

Ans. Yes, a joint family is a happy family because members start developing a mutual understanding towards one another but at the same time joint family is not happy family these days because the generation gap between the parents and children plays a vital role because the person who comes into our family can't cope up with our family as our parents want him/her to do something and he/she will not be ready to bear any restriction.

5. **What are some tips which can help in a strong bonding family?**

Ans. To develop a strong bond requires tremendous support and understanding among family members. You should give value to the opinion even given by the smallest member. No one should be underestimated. Event or activity give positive feedback so play card or board games of their choices. Watch a TV program that your kids like. Have a family night out and go to a movie, concert etc.

6. **What are the responsibilities of the family so they keep themselves united and undivided?**

Ans. A united and undivided family is like a fortress. It gives you solidarity, strength and cooperation. Every member of such family has some obligation that will keep the root cemented. It should be the duty of the Karta of the family to warm all the misgivings. All the children are to be given the same food, education and environment. All members of the family have their meals at the same time and place. All the earnings of the family should be funneled in a central fund. All the problems facing the family should be discussed at length with all the members and a decision be reached. An unanimous decision is all the better.

7. **What is close knit family?**

Ans. A close – knit family is such a family in which all the members have strong bonding with others. Communication between family members is the main thing in a close knit family. When there is communication gap, the family is no longer can be considered as a close knit family. The family which eats together, lives together, laughs together and shares all trials and tribulations together is a Close Knit Family.

8. **How can family problems affect your behaviour in life?**

Ans. It is often observed in many cases that family problems always create mental problems in life and has been universally observed in almost every household. Where is family, there is problem and family problem is common in world. And too many problems that make you upset and create tension and stress. So to keep oneself steady and firm one should be determined firm and steady to face the situation.

9. **Do you think respect is the foundation of happy family?**

Ans. Yes, Respect is the foundation of all the relation out there and no one can build relations without respect for one another. Every family has to adopt certain norms and values which treats them to respect their elders but unfortunately, their values and norms have lost its gleam in the present materialistic' world.

10. **What are the responsibilities of a son towards the family?**

Ans. The son's position in the family is to follow the traditions and heritage, to be respectful to the elders, to learn from the elders experience, to keep complications at bay, to keep life full of humour, and to orient the path of youngsters. One must be a care taker of his family as well as the society and one benefit from his family culture and environment and last but not least, he should maintain dignity and must respect his belongings.

Practice Questions

1. Are joint families better than nuclear families?
2. Is love important or families?
3. What do you think of your family? Do you compare your family with other family?
4. Is it possible for the head of the family to please everyone in the family?
5. What do you understand by an ideal family?
6. Will you go against your family anytime in any matter?
7. Why are young people in today's world least bothered about relationships in the family?

ABSTRACT

SPEAKING TEST

Here, we are providing some solved/unsolved sample papers for IELTS speaking test for the convenience of the students. It covers all the three sections i.e. interview Session; Cue Card Explanation and Follow Up session.

SPEAKING TEST – 1

SOLVED

1. **Good afternoon. My name is Andy could you tell me your name please?**

Ans. _______________ Thank you.

a. **What are you doing presently?**

Ans. I am doing a job in a multi-national company as an Administrative Executive Officer.

b. **What is your academic qualification?**

Ans. I am post graduate in Master of Business Administration from a reputed university of Pune.

c. **Do you keep goals in your mind for the future?**

Ans. I prefer short-term goals because these types of goals give stress-free, flexible and practical approach to wards work which unlimitedly increases my work and efficiency.

d. **What do you usually eat for breakfast?**

Ans. Actually sir, I am a very health conscious man. I take very light breakfast like citrus fruit juices, sometimes porridge, or sometimes bread and milk.

e. **According to your opinion, what is life?**

Ans. According to me, life is *not a bed of roses,* rather it is a *bed of thorns* where everybody has to struggle in order to sustain.

f. **Do you believe kith and kin play important role in our lives?**

Ans. Sir or Madam, as we know, no man can live in insolation. Everybody needs some kind of social relationship, may it be in the form of parents, friends or relatives but according to my opinion, nowadays, with the influence of materialism, money is everything. Nobody bothers about any kind of good relationship.

g. **Do you like flowers?**

Ans. Of course, yes, I like almost all the flowers like rose, sunflower and all other exotic flowers because they not only give fragrance but their vibrant colours also refresh our minds.

h. What kind of people do you like in your life?

Ans. I like self-esteemed, vibrant, honest, courageous and god loving people. These kind of people who have a positive attitude towards life and believe in hard work. Imitative are my role models.

2. **Now I am going to give you a topic and I like you to speak on it for 1-2 minutes.**

You have one minute to prepare your answer.

Here is your topic.

Describe your favourite website.

You should say

Name of the Website

When you came to know about it

How often you visit it

What you like about the Website

The website I visit almost every day is google.com.

This portal is one of the best websites in the world. Therefore, I opened my e-mail account with this website in 2000 and since then, I have been visiting this site regularly. This site offers a very powerful and comprehensive search engine through which we can search for information about any websites or web pages. This site offers numerous communication services for their users across the world like e-mails, messengers and chat services. Nowadays, this website also offers radio and international calling service.

In addition to it, it also offers various online communication belonging to different interests in the form of blogs and groups so that we can share and gain knowledge in the subject of our interest. Other websites like yahoo.com, rediffmail.com are providing very unlimited search services. But this site offers every graphical, images, etc. interface search services. Nowadays this site has become more friendly with the help of social networking sites like facebook, twitter, etc. I like this site the most and it has become an indispensable part of my life.

Follow up Questions

1. **What other websites do you visit?**

Ans. I visit yahoo.com, rediffmail, sify and some portals related to matrimonial sites.

2. **How many hours a day do you use Internet?**

Ans. I usually spend 3 to 4 hours a day on the Internet.

3. We've been talking about websites, internet and computer, and I'd like to ask you a few questions related to computer and Internet.

a. Do you use a computer?

Ans. Yes, of course, I am fond of computers. I usually complete my home tasks, office work and other activities on computer. It makes my life faster accurate and infact, complete.

b. What do you mean by the word, 'E' in computer?

Ans. 'E' stands for electronic. In computer, this word gaining its ground day by day. Nowadays, there is e-teaching, e-education, e-cards, e-mails, e-chat, e-communication etc. So I can say this word has converted the global world into a small village.

c. What are the advantages and disadvantages of e-learning?

Ans. E-learning opens up the doors of education across the globe. It makes the study possible for those who cannot attend classes because they don't have time for that. In addition, it also provides a platform for individual development because students cannot get everyday support from their tutors but the major drawback of this type of learning for those candidates who can't cope up with the study requirements. For those candidates it's just a one-way traffic.

d. What are your views regarding smart card technology in various institutions like schools and colleges?

Ans. Smart card technology is one of the astonishing inventions of technology which is being implemented these days in different institutions, schools and colleges. This type of technology not only gives a practical, sound and logical approach to the students but also enhances their exposure and empirical level of study. They become more analytical and logical with the use of this technology.

e. Why are old people reluctant in accepting and using computers?

Ans. This happens because of conservative and outdated outlook among these people but no doubt the introduction of computer can bring radical change in that set up which also pushes those elders to changes their ideas and views.

f. What do you think will be the future of computers?

Ans. I think our lives will become impossible without computers. Nowadays it not only makes our life faster and accurate, but it also teaches us moral values of life through artificial intelligence. So without it, life will be a body without flesh and blood.

Thank you. This is the end of the Speaking Test 1.

SPEAKING TEST – 2

SOLVED

1. **Good afternoon, my name is Angline. Could you tell me your full name please? What should I call you' Thank you.**

   a. **Do you work, or are you a student?**

   Ans. I am a student.

   b. **Can you tell me about your studies?**

   Ans. I am pursuing my graduation studies these days.

   c. **What are your leisure time activities?**

   Ans. My leisure time activities are reading books, listening to soft music and surfing on the internet for the websites offering knowledge on various creative and learning skills

   d. **What leisure activities according to you will be popular in the future?**

   Ans. It is difficult to say but I think activities based on technology like playing 3 – dimensional or virtual reality games, chatting and browsing on the net, etc., will be highly popular in the future.

   e. **What do you prefer more, homemade food or restaurant food, and why?**

   Ans. I prefer homemade food because every day, it is not possible for me to go to the the restaurants. Moreover, I love to eat homemade food because it is more hygienic than restaurant food.

   f. **What is hygienic food?**

   Ans. Food which is rich in nutrients like vitamins, minerals, protein and carbohydrates, and are without germs is called hygienic food.

   g. **Is there any food which you don't like?**

   Ans. I don't like to eat too much spicy and non-vegetarian food because it is harmful for our digestive system.

   h. **Do you think food reflects our culture?**

   Ans. Food is actually a part of our culture. Infact, it is the mirror of our culture. For example, the chinese people eat noodles in India. Different states are known by their foods like Punjabi people are famous for their diet like *Sarso ka Saag* and *Makke ki roti, Gujaratis Eat Dhokla*, etc.

2. **Now I am going to give you a topic and I like you to speak on it for 1-2 minutes. You have one minute to prepare your answer. Here is your topic**

   Describe about your Mobile Phone you use regularly.

As we are witnessing tremendous revolution in the communication sector in the last decade, here I would like to speak about my mobile phone which I use regularly. Mobile phones multi-dimensional gadget. It not only works as a phone have but it also serves having e-mail facility, camera, internet, SMS, MMS, bluetooth, animation, etc. So, with different colours, become this communication gadget plays an indispensable role in our daily's lives. I use the phone to talk to my family, friends, relatives, students and colleague. Sometimes, I am not able to attend my phone calls. But at that time, my phone has a box stores all my calls in a call log. In mobile phones, we can maintain our pocket telephone dairy.

Moreover, short message services are useful to me when I want to convey text or graphics to other mobile phones. I can also check my e-mails in my mobile. In addition to all these, my mobile gives me the facility of an alarm clock, daily planner, currency converter, world time and games. Hence in today's busy and commercial life, a mobile has become an essential instrument for all people in the world.

3. **Now I'd like to ask you a few more questions about communication and technology sector.**

a. **What are the advantages and disadvantages of a mobile phone?**

Ans. A mobile phone offers many benefits like fast and easy communication with anyone at anytime, storing, sending, and receiving data like phone numbers, music and photos. However it has some drawbacks too. It can be misused in a number of ways like SMS, MMS and Viruses. Also, it takes our privacy away as anyone can trace us easily. Moreover, doctors recommend that mobile phones are harmful for the heart and the brain also

b. **What are the important inventions of the century?**

Ans. There have been countless inventions in the last hundred years. Inventions in the field of technology are radio, television, aeroplanes, satellites, space travel, computers, mobile internet, and presently, tablets are famous with its features of Android and Whatsapp.

c. **How does technology influence the field of communication?**

Ans. Technology plays an indispensable role in the field of communication. It helps us to stay in touch with anyone at anytime, quickly and safely by sending and receiving important documents in the electronic form. Moreover, people these days use video – conferencing to meet their colleagues who are in different parts of the world. Technology is the heart of business and communication.

d. **Do you think a country progresses if technology progresses?**

Ans. Yeah, the country will progress by the leaps and bounds with the progress of science and technology, as it serves as the growth engine of the economy. The country can have better industrial and agricultural ground with reduced cost input with the help of science and technology. As a result, the country exports these products to other international companies and consequently, the GDP of the country rises which is the sign of a growing economy.

e. **According to you, what is the future of technology?**

Ans. According to my opinion, only technology retains in future life. As we are living the era of nuclear world, So if any country has to survive in this era, they are under obligation to accept technology for making their arms and ammunition.

f. **What are destructive uses of technology?**

Ans. The destructive uses of technology are in Weapons, Nuclear, Energy, Laser and other destructive weapons which are capable of destroying the earth completely if they go into wrong hands

Thank you. This is the end of your Speaking Test 2.

SPEAKING TEST – 3

SOLVED

1. **Good afternoon, My Name is Reena. Could you tell me your full name please Name of the candidate. Thank You.**

a. **Do you work or are you a student?**

Ans. I am working as an executive manager.

b. **What difficulties did you face in your first job interview?**

Ans. I was little bit nervous during the time of my first job interview. I knew nothing about the company, as it was a walk-in-interview. Many candidates appeared in it which made me even more skeptical about my selection. However, I performed well and I was shortlisted by the interviewing panel for a personal interview. Finally, I got an appointment letter after a few days of my interview.

c. **Why do you prefer job to business?**

Ans. No doubt, Business gives freedom to experiment and explore new ideas. It also gives us the independent decision and managing power. But job offers us security and less stressful life because job gives a fixed salary.

d. **What are your strengths that help you in your current job?**

Ans. Ah! My hard work, initiation, efficient leadership, vibrant attitude, and last but not the least, dedication towards my work help me and a lot in my current job.

e. **What types of jobs do males and females prefer?**

Ans. Males prefer jobs that require some travelling, as youngsters like to travel and learn practical lessons of life, while females prefer office jobs likethat of a receptionist, computer operator, telephone operator, telecaller, secretary, etc.

f. **Should college students do part-time job? Why?**

Ans. Of course why not. College students must do part-time job because it helps them to earn money. Moreover, they become more responsible, matured and self-reliant by doing jobs.

g. **In which jobs do employees have to update themselves regularly?**

Ans. All types of jobs require regular updating, but there are still some jobs like medicine IT, software programming media jobs, etc. which require faster up-to-date knowledge from professionals.

h. **What are the ways to search for jobs?**

Ans. There are three ways to search for jobs. First, we can look for advertisements in the newspapers and apply for the jobs. Second, we can consult with placement consultants. Third, we can apply for online jobs in portals.

2. **Now I'd like to ask you to speak for 1-2 minutes on a topic. You have one minute to plan your answer. Here is your topic**

Describe your favourite time of the day.

You should say:

What time of the day it is

What you do during this time

Why that time is your favourite

No doubt every moment of the day of my life is precious to me. However, the time I enjoy the most during the day is the early morning. I like the morning time because at that time, I am completely fresh, and prepared to take on a new day. I go out of my home for a short walk. While walking, I feel fresh, and its very soothing in the pollution-free air. Then I walk on grass to keep my eyes healthy and all these things help me a lot to stay fresh, full of energy and promising. After that, I also prepare my day's schedule in my mind. I have selected this time for preparation of my daily routine. So the morning time, acts as a blue print for the whole day to come.

Follow up Questions

1. **Why don't some people change their routine life?**

Ans. Some People don't change their routine life due to lack of restiveness among them. They don't want to bring change in their life. They shirk from varietyful lives, but it is wrong. Change is the law of nature. One should change according to one's time and circumstances.

2. **Are habits and hobbies dependent on the routine of a person?**

Ans. No, not at all. Because routine means disciplined life, where habits and hobbies are the activities of leisure time. So, habits and hobbies are not dependant on the routine of person.

3. Now I'd like to ask you a few more questions related to your daily life.

a. **How are hobbies useful to us?**

Ans. Hobbies are useful to us in many ways. We can pass our time in a creative manner which helps us in gaining expertise on other areas of life.

b. **Don't you think hobbies are a wastage of time?**

Ans. No, not at all. It is rather it is a creative utilisation of our time. By pursuing hobbies, we can actually pull out our hidden abilities and talents which are very important for our all round development.

c. **What are the benefits of laughing?**

Ans. Laughing offers immense benefits. When we laugh our mind relaxes and we feel fresh. It is a common saying, "Laughter is the best medicine." Those who laugh have higher immunity and are less likely to suffer from any disease.

d. **Do you think time management is a useful tool to improve your efficiency?**

Ans. Time management teaches us the skills to give the desired priority to the tasks in hand. Time is very precious, so that it should not be wasted in useless things. It is necessary that we can schedule our time and can make the best use of it.

e. **What was best time of your childhood?**

Ans. The best time of my childhood days was when I was in school. We used to play a lot of games and fight with one another over small things. Actually, the childhood days were without stress and tensions. One enjoys every moment of it with full fervour and excitement.

f. **How do you manage disputes in your friendship?**

Ans. True friendship is beyond disputes. However, if we have any misunderstanding or communication gap, we first meet with each other and clarify everything. Yet, if we reach on irrecoverable situation, we always try our best by keeping other's benefit in mind.

Thank you. This is the end of your Speaking Test.

PRACTICE SPEAKING TEST – 4

SOLVED

1. **Good afternoon, My name is Debra. May I check your identifications please? Thank you.**

   a. Do you believe in God?

   Ans. Yes, I do rather I am a God-loving and a God-fearing person.

   b. What is your favourite colour?

   Ans. I love the *green colour* because it is a *symbol of prosperity* and it always creates a cheerful atmosphere in the surroundings.

   c. What is the importance of education in our lives?

   Ans. Education provides an unflinching support to our skills and knowledge to survive, grow and support our family and the society. According to me, it is the fuel for growth and the supportive engine of the world.

   d. Do you think practical knowledge should be given during college days?

   Ans. Yes, it is essential to give practical training to the students because without practical knowledge, students get familiar only with the bookish world which can create problems for them when they face the real world.

   e. What personality traits should be kept in mind when one has to achieve success in life/business?

   Ans. There are many qualities needed to get success in life and business. Some of them are vibrant attitude, persistence, honesty, hard work, competitiveness, ability to envisage future outcomes and so on.

   f. According to you, which life is better, school life or college life?

   Ans. According to my opinion, both lives have their own special significance. But for me, college life is much better because at college, we come out of the innocent world of school and enter the world of independence and adulthood.

   g. Do you like to attend parties, discotheques/dance floors?

   Ans. Yeah, I do like them, but occasionally.

   h. Which days do you celebrate with your family?

   Ans. I celebrate birthdays, anniversaries and all achievements in my life with my family members. I celebrate such events mostly with my family, but we do invite our friends and relatives for celebration on a larger-scale, sometimes.

2. **Now I'd like to ask you to speak for 1-2 minutes on a topic you have one minute to plan your answer.**

Here is your topic

Describe your favourite theatre

Name and location

How often you visit it

What you like about it

Watching or going to cinema is one of my favourite recreational activities. I like 'PVR' the most popular multiplex in my city. This is actually a first multiple which opened with grand cinemas in our city. All six screens show different movies at different timings so that they offer a wide variety to the viewers. It has both lifts and escalators for the visitors to move easily in the complex. The whole building offers a lot of options like discotheque, games zone, shopping section, food court, book shop and so one. This building has an innovative interior design. It is constructed in such a way that we can have the visibility of all the corners of the building as we come to the central part of the building. The cinema halls are different in size, but are very good in ambience. They are well air-conditioned, have comfortable seats and excellent sound system. All these facilities make movie watching a pleasurable experience. In addition, they also offer online ticket-booking and free home delivery of tickets for customers. I think it is a complete package of recreation and entertainment.

Follow up Questions

1. **Do you like to visit cinema halls regularly?**

Ans. No, but I love to watch the first day first show of the latest movies.

2. **If you are given a choice, what would you prefer, watching a drama or a movie and why?**

Ans. Both have their own attractions. Drama is a live performance of actors on the stage, and hence it is more alive and involving. It is a challenging task for the performers because they don't get retakes in a drama. So, for lovers of acting and live performance, drama is a better choice. However, movies offer us better sound effects, cinematography and music. I often opt for movies because I like to watch different outdoor locations, newer costumes and innovative storylines.

3. **Now I'd like to ask you a few more questions related to your family.**

   a. **What changes have you seen in the family system in the last decade?**

   Ans. Nuclear families and small families are gaining grounds in a large proportion in the society. However, a reverse trend is also visible in some countryside areas of my nation, where all the members of the family live together under one roof.

   b. **What are the positive and negative points of living in a joint family?**

   Ans. Joint family offers love, affection, sharing warmth and unity. During trials and tribulations of life, only joint families prove to be boon. Moreover, cultural legacy can be easily passed on to the next generations in joint families. On the other hand, there is a lack of privacy in joint families at times. Moreover, these types of families are easily proned to conflicts and consensus.

c. **What is the importance of family in your life?**

Ans. Family is the first school where our society develops. It is a set up, where we can live a natural life without playing any psychological games with one another that we normally play outside our families. In other, words, a family is the base of our life where the pyramid of our nature stands.

d. **What are the reasons behind breaking down of joint families into nuclear families?**

Ans. The prime reason for this is economical development. Because of this, people started shifting to bigger and industrial cities from small towns and villages. It is obvious that when we migrate, we cannot shift as a joint family in the beginning, and hence, families break and live in different places of the country.

e. **Do you think today's family members show less warmth and feelings compared to the past?**

Ans. I don't agree with this. I do accept that changes have taken place in our life styles and this doesn't allow family members to give enough time to one another. But it doesn't mean that they have less respect and feelings for one another. It is a common saying, blood is thicker than water. It doesn't need time to strengthen them. Family bindings are always stronger and are beyond such requirements.

SPEAKING TEST – 5

SOLVED

1. **Good afternoon my name is Rowdy. May I check your identification please? Thank you.**

a. **Which games/sports are popular in your country?**

Ans. Popular games/sports of my country are Cricket, Hockey, Football, Tennis, Table Tennis, Billiards, Volleyball and Badminton. However, the most popular games/sports among all is the Cricket. I can say that cricket is not just a game but a religion in India, as people are obsessed with this game throughout, the nation.

b. **Do women get an equal opportunity to participate in all games in your country?**

Ans. Yes, women get equal opportunities to participate in all games in our country, both at the national and international levels.

c. **What is the importance of religion in our lives?**

Ans. Religion acts as a mirror in our lives. Through meditation or following any religion, we get eternal peace, satisfaction and happiness in life.

d. **What can we learn from religious people?**

Ans. We can understand various aspects of our religion and our lives, which we can implement in our everyday living. If we have any problem in our lives, we can go to them and seek the necessary solutions from the religious perspectives. They are an important part of our lives.

e. **What do you think about student teacher relationship?**

Ans. I think a student-teacher relationship must be *friendly and interactive*. It is very important for both of them to understand each other to ensure smoothness in the learning process. If there is a distance in the teacher-student relationship, the learning becomes difficult and disturbed which cannot give the desired results to the students.

f. **Why do people want to study/settle in other countries?**

Ans. Actually, foreign education gives international exposure to the students which help them to begin their professional lives. Moreover, countries like Australia offer settlement options to overseas students. That's why many people want to study/ settle in other countries.

g. **Do you think the modern generation ignores elders?**

Ans. In some families, a generation gap is seen among youngsters and parents due to different tastes, ideas and education. This is just because of the influence of western culture. However, it is not true for most families and still in some families, morals play an indispensable role.

h. **What makes you happy in life?**

Ans. Everything that is good for me, my family my friends etc. I don't believe in a conditional and emotional response to the situation in my life. I believe that contentment towards life brings eternal happiness.

2. **Now I'd like to ask you to speak for 1-2 minutes on a topic. You have one minute to plan your answer. Here is your topic.**

Describe your favourite Radio program

Name of the program

When it is broadcasted

What the program is all about

MY FAVOURITE RADIO PROGRAM

Radio FM is an audio media player. Nowadays, it offers an astonishing entertainment to the listeners. It is not the invention of new technology rather it is an 'old wine in new bottles'. I love to hear, "DIL SE LOVE GURU" program at 'FM DIL SE' at 11.00 pm. This program is hosted by everyday by Love Guru, Supreet. Really, he is very adventurous and adorable person. The way he solves the love problems and brings happiness in the lives of people is really remarkable. I love his joking style also. He not only solves problems, but also entertains us with exotic songs. He tells love percentages of different couples from his love meter. He is blessed with a good voice gainful grounds, I think god has gifted him, "The gift of the gab". Now-days, he opens "Diljale Club" or "Making friends Club" for helping persons in trouble. This program is broadcasted for two hours from Monday to Friday. Through this program, we can send our warm wishes to our friend, share, our emotions and feelings with our soulmates, etc. I like this program very much.

Follow up Questions

1. Is the popularity of radio increasing or decreasing these days? Why?

Ans. The popularity of radio has increased a lot in the last few years in my country because of the entry of private companies with FM (Frequency Modulation) channels on radio.

2. What are the advantages offered by the radio over TV?

Ans. Radio offers some benefits over television. It is an audio-media player and thus, it can be taken anywhere and enjoyed what is more. People now have radio in their mobiles which provides entertainment their fingertips. All these facilities are not offered by television because it requires a big screen.

3. Now I'd like to ask you a few more questions related to the media, radio and television?

a. What is the main function of the media?

Ans. The media is a medium of mass communication which provides information to a big mass of people who can access it and use the knowledge for their benefits.

b. What are the basic responsibilities of the media?

Ans. The media is a platform of gaining knowledge, information's and entertainment. So the moral responsibility of the media is to be independent, free and impartial. It should create appropriate awareness among the masses instead of misguiding them.

c. Do you think the media is helpful in our lives?

Ans. Yes, the media is very helpful and beneficial to our lives. It updates our knowledge about politics, financial matters, education, business, jobs, management, fashion, lifestyles, etc.

d. When do you listen to your favourite radio program?

Ans. Actually. I am a very busy person, but I still spend some time to listen to my favourite radio program. I usually listen at 10.00 pm, when I go for sleep.

Thank you. This is the end of Practice Speaking Test

PRACTICE SPEKING TEST – 1

1. **Good Morning, Hey this is Gaby. Could you tell me your full name please?**
   a. Do you work, or are you a student?
   b. What is your future plan?
   c. Why are you taking IELTS?
   d. Do you think struggle is necessary to achieve something in your life?
   e. What are the initiatives performed by a struggling man to achieve his goals?
   f. What are your smart skills?
   g. What will you do to improve your smart skills?
   h. Do you have any personal ambitions?
2. **Describe three things which you hope to achieve in your life**
   you should say.
   What are those three things
   Why have you chosen these three things
   How you will achieve it
   And explain, how these three things plays an indispensable role in other's life.
3. (a) What are these threee things through which a common man gets identification and recognition?
   (b) Do you believe in the identity of a common man?
   (c) What are the attributes of a luxurious life?
   (d) Do you feel people who are living a luxurious life are living hurdle a free life?
   (e) What will you do to earn name, fame and money?
   (f) What is the most impossible thing in today's life?

Thank you. This is the end of Practice Speaking Test – 1

PRACTICE SPEAKING TEST – 2

1. **Good Morning. I'm Taffy. May I check your identification please?**
   a. Do you like Internet surfing?
   b. How does surfing help you?
   c. Do you have your own web portal or an e-mail account?
   d. Which software do you like the most? And why?
   e. Do you think surfing is good for children?
   f. What will be the future of computer?
   g. Which is the most interesting feature of the Internet that appeals you?
   h. How much time do you spend on the Internet daily?
2. **Describe your Facebook account on the Internet.**
   You should say:
   - The name of your Facebook account
   - Why you chose the Facebook
   - Where it is
   - How it brings a change into your life, and also explain why this has lot of craze among the teenagers of India?
3. a. Do you like the Twitter or the Facebook and why?
   b. Why do people publicize themselves through the Facebook?
   c. Does Facebook bring any remarkable change in your life?
   d. "Facebook harms your personal secrecy" How far do you agree with this statement?
   e. Do you think the Facebook is a short-cut way to earn publicity?

Thank you. This is the end of Practice Speaking Test– 2

PRACTICE SPEAKING TEST – 3

1. **Good Morning. My name is Madeline. Could you tell me your full name please?**
    a. Do you work, or are you a student?
    b. What do you like about your work?
    c. What are the skills required for your profession?
    d. Do you think 'English' plays an important role in handling your job?
    e. How should a candidate prepare himself/herself in order to get success in a job interview?
    f. If you are given a chance to go abroad, which country would you like to visit and why?
    g. Do you enjoy discotheques?
    h. How would you like to spend your weekends?
2. **Describe your reasons for choosing your particular course of study.**

    You should say:
    - Name of the course
    - Why have you chosen this course
    - From where are you getting the coaching
    - Also explain, how this course will orient you towards your ambition in life?
3. a. Do you believe in Astrology?
    b. Is there any important number in your culture?
    c. Do you think today's people are inclined more towards superstitious numbers?
    d. How can we eradicate superstitions?
    e. What are the ill effects of superstitious ness?

Thank you. This is the end of Practice Speaking Test – 3

PRACTICE SPEAKING TEST – 4

1. **Good Morning. I am Gabby.**
   a. Could you tell me your full name please?
   b. May I know about your academic qualifications?
   c. Does your education help you in anyway in your present life?
   d. Do you think today, for parents, educating their children in good schools is a big issue for them?
   e. What type of learning method suit you the best?
   f. What are your duties towards your parents?
   g. What is essential for parents to teach their children?
2. **Describe any feature of the education system of your country**
   You should say:
   - What it is
   - Why you find it interesting
   - What makes it important and noteworthy

   And say, how this feature might be used elsewhere
3. a. Do you think smart classes is the best for the students?
   b. What skills are required for smart class learning?
   c. Do you think smart class is harmful for the teacher-student relationship?
   d. What are the basic ingredients to learn in your educational system?
   e. Can you suggest some ways to reform educational system?

Thank you. This is the end of Practice Speaking Test – 4

PRACTICE SPEAKING TEST – 5

1. **Good Morning my, name is Tom. May I check your identification please?**
   a. Do you live in a village or town? Why do you like it?
   b. What is your occupation?
   c. What do you prefer more, homemade food or restaurant food and why?
   d. Do you like to eat junk food?
   e. Should we completely ban non-vegetarian food? Yes or No and why?
   f. Nowadays there is a mad craze among youngsters for fad diets? Do you prefer such diet?
   g. Why do most of the girls prefer to go on dieting instead of doing exercise?
   h. Do you think 'Yoga' will protect your life from disease?
2. **Describe your favourite sweet dish**
   You should say:
   - Name of the dish
   - Why you like it
   - Who made it, and explain which ingredients make it sweet?

   a. Which is more important for you health or wealth and why?
   b. What do you understand by nutritious food?
   c. Is it advisable to go for a regular body checkup?
   d. What type of exercises do help you the most in maintaining the health, according to you?
   e. Do you think by joining, 'Healthcare Centres' we can maintain our health?

Thank you. This is the end of Practice Speaking Test – 5

PRACTICE SPEAKING TEST – 6

1. **Good Afternoon, I am Garry Swift. Take your seat please.**
   a. What are your hobbies?
   b. How are your hobbies useful to you?
   c. How many languages do you prefer to write?
   d. Do you like to visit discotheques?
   e. Tell me something about your hometown?
   f. What types of facilities will be available in the future house?
   g. What is the special feature of your city?
   h. Do you feel homesick when you are sitting far from your family?
2. **Describe an ideal house'**
   You should say:
   - Why do you prefer this kind of house
   - What are its accommodation facilities
   - Where it is located
   - How it fulfills the need of your family

   a. Tell me, what are the basic attractions of your hometown?
   b. Do you feel that your hometown needs any improvements?
   c. What type of schools and colleges are there in your town?
   d. Is your hometown free from pollution problem?
   e. What measures are adopted by the government officials in improving your home town?

Thank you. This is the end of Practice Speaking Test – 6

PRACTICE SPEAKING TEST – 7

1. **Hey, this is Mady. Could you tell me your full name, please?**
   a. Are you married or not?
   b. Is wedding necessary in life?
   c. Are you willing to marry according to your parent's wish or you want to marry according to your own wish?
   d. What difficulties can an unmarried individual face at the later stage of life?
   e. Which is better according to you? Love marriage or arranged marriage? Why?
   f. What qualities are necessary to lead the best marriageable life?
   g. According to you, what is an exact age for marriage in today's world?
2. **Tell me something about the ideal relationship in your life.**
   - Name of the relation
   - Why it is ideal for you
   - How it influence and brings happiness to your life.
3. a. Do you consult your family members/spouse, while making an important decision?
   b. Do you believe that decisions made in haste are always wrong?
   c. What skills are required to take decisions?
   d. What important decisions are you going to make for your future?
   e. Do you help others in taking their decisions?

Thank you. This is the end of Practice Speaking Test -7

PRACTICE SPEAKING TEST – 8

1. **Hello I'm Madaline. May I check your identification please?**
   a. Who is your best friend?
   b. How did this friend become your bosom friend?
   c. Do you feel your friend stands with you in all trials and tribulations of your life?
   d. What kind of food do you enjoy eating?
   e. Does your friend's habits match with your parents?
   f. Tell me something about the social conditions of your hometown?
   g. Do you feel that there is exploitation of women at working places in your hometown?
   h. Is child labour still persistent in your town?
2. **Describe one of the major problem of your country.**
   You should say:
   - Which problem it is
   - What are its roots
   - How it disturbs the humanity

   And explain, the cause of its expansion
3. a. What are the activities performed by the terrorists to disturb the masses?
   b. Do you think we should have a terrorist control cell in our society?
   c. What are the social problems of your country?
   d. Tell me how can media help overcoming the problems of your country?
   e. What reforms do you suggest to improve the conditions of your country?

Thank you. This is the end of Practice Speaking Test – 8

PRACTICE SPEAKING TEST – 9

1. **Good Morning, please take your seat.**
   a. Do you play any sports?
   b. Do you think sports keep you healthy?
   c. Can sports be dangerous for a diseased man?
   d. How do you enjoy your weekends?
   e. Are you fond of travelling?
   f. How do you spend your Sundays?
   g. What activities do you not perform on Sundays which you do during week days?
   h. Why are 'Sundays' special for everybody?
2. **Describe your favourite sport**
   - Which sport it is
   - Why do you like it
   - Where do you practise it and explain how it proves to be a thrill and adventurous for you
3. a. Do you play at the national or international level?
   b. In your country, which games are popular, indoor games or outdoor games?
   c. Can media promote sportsmanship?
   d. How does a sportperson overcome his fatigue?
   e. What are the qualities that make you a good sportsman?

Thank you. This is the end of Practice Speaking Test – 9

PRACTICE SPEAKING TEST – 10

1. **Good Morning, Please take your seat.**
   a. From which college did you complete your graduation?
   b. Is your city good for youngsters?
   c. Could you describe your college life?
   d. Do you think co-ed colleges are the best then single sex colleges and why?
   e. Why is eve-teasing raising its heads in your locality?
   f. What will you do when you come across eve-teasing in you locality?
   g. Who is responsible for eve-teasing?
   h. Do you think sex education should be impaired in school?
2. **Ragging should be banned. Do you agree or not?**
   You should say:
   - Act of indiscipline
   - How it affects our culture
   - What are the government's step to curb it
3. **a. Do you feel private students are better than college going? Why?**
   b. What are the basic requirements to be a collegiate?
   c. Colleges are the basic arena for the evolution of politics. How far do you agree?
   d. What type of vocational courses are running in colleges these days?
   e. Do you think doing graduation from a college is sufficient for getting a job?

Thank you. This is the end of Practice Speaking Test – 10